EXPLOSIVE
SEX!

THIS IS A CARLTON BOOK

Design and special photography copyright © Carlton Books
Limited 2011
Text © Richard Emerson 2011

This paperback edition published in 2011
by Carlton Books Limited
20 Mortimer Street
London W1T 3JW

10 9 8 7 6 5 4 3 2 1

ISBN 978 1 84732 864 9

Printed and bound in Hong Kong

Senior Executive Editor: Lisa Dyer
Managing Art Director: Lucy Coley
Designer: Barbara Zuñiga
Production: Kate Pimm
Hair and Makeup: Johanna Dalemo
Photographer: Laura Knox
Models: Spencer, Leah, Aimee and Leon,
all at International Model Management London

EXPLOSIVE
SEX!

step-by-step techniques
for the hottest sex ever

Richard Emerson

CONTENTS

INTRODUCTION

"Love is not the dying moan of a distant violin.
It is the triumphant twang of a bedspring."
S. J. Perelman

Light the blue touch paper and retire… to bed.
If more couples could enjoy satisfyingly intense, orgasmic explosive sex, like a rocket shooting into the sky with an earth-shaking whoosh, then maybe fewer relationships would sputter out like a soggy squib. Of course, relationships fail for many reasons, but some of the most common causes lie in the bedroom. Some couples find they no longer share the same sexual needs and desires, for example, or that their sexual relationship has lost its spark. Others come to believe that their lovemaking is never going to hit the orgasmic heights they had hoped for and so they've simply stopped trying.

All break-ups are tragic, but none more so than those that could be saved with a little more imagination and (dare I say) risk-taking between the sheets. If you reckon your love life needs more whiz and (especially) bang, then this book can help. Think of it as a firework fiesta for lovers – like a bonfire party that sets your libido alight and sends your passion racing into the stratosphere. It is packed with great ideas for fun and frolics in the bedroom, or anywhere else in the house that takes your fancy.

What kind of lover are you? Do you sizzle like a Chinese firecracker, or smoulder like a Roman candle? Perhaps you're a scintillating sparkler that dazzles with desire? In the following pages, our guide to *Your Sexual Personality* reveals all. You'll find sex profiles based on star signs, plus tips for risqué romps to suit your nature. Turn to the relevant page to try them out.

No matter how you're feeling, there are lots of ways to nurture the warm glow of romance. You'll find sinful suggestions in Chapter 1 – *Petting & Foreplay* that are guaranteed to kindle any couple's

passion. If you're in a party mood and think laughter's the best aphrodisiac, then start with Chapter 3 – *Fun & Games* – for a list of perky pastimes only lovers play – especially when they're young at heart.

For the most excitingly X-rated activities, however, see the *Explosive Sex Sequences*. Here you'll find sexy moves designed to vary, heighten and extend your lovemaking more than you ever imagined and send your climax off the Richter scale. If you're already in a heightened state of arousal and can't wait a second longer to try something new then don't delay – turn to the Chapter 2 today!

This book is designed to be informative and fun, rather than a scholarly work of medical science. Yet the information it contains is based on up-to-date scientific research into the physical, emotional and psychological nature of lovemaking, as well as in-depth studies involving real couples (every one of them a willing volunteer!). Sex therapists and relationship counsellors base their advice on such research when helping couples overcome sexual problems and keep their relationship alive.

Throughout this book (and those secret searches on the Internet when you thought no one was watching) you'll come across sexual terms with which you may be unfamiliar. There is a handy glossary at the back of the book to help you get to the bottom of things, as it were. It may even introduce you to parts of your body you never knew you had! So keep a mirror handy and study them at your leisure.

If you think of your love life as a firework, then view this book as the slow match that sets it alight and sends it soaring skywards to produce a spectacular starburst of sexual satisfaction. Explosive sex indeed…

YOUR SEXUAL PERSONALITY…
AS REVEALED IN THE STARS

We all have romantic moments, but other times we can be so overcome
with raw passion that we just want to rip our partner's clothes off.
there and then. So what is your true sexual nature? Are you naturally
adventurous, romantic, passionate, shy, dominant or submissive? Our
sexual personality guide may help you to discover more about
yourself… and your partner.

The 12 personalities described here are based on the signs of the
zodiac. Not everyone believes that sexual nature is determined by star
date, but you may recognize some features that match your own and
those of your lover. If you would rather be a passionate Leo than a
romantic Libran, however, perhaps now is the time to change. Simply
identify the star sign you'd like to be in the bedroom and read on
for some steamy suggestions to help you make the transformation.

ARIES (*21 March – 20 April*)

Sexual profile: This is a fire sign and Arians have the personality to match. Fearless, impulsive and alive to new challenges, the bedroom is the last place you'll find yourself with an Arian. They prefer spontaneous moments of passion under a table, in a cupboard, behind a tree, standing up or upside down. Expect Arian lovers to take charge and suggest something outrageous.

Sexual match: Aquarius, Libra.

Sexual preferences: Standing sex, rear-entry sex, al fresco sex and fun and games.

TAURUS (*21 April – 21 May*)

Sexual profile: Sensual by nature, expect those born under this earth sign to be secretive, introverted and conservative yet with hidden depths like an untapped mine. Taureans hate being rushed but once roused burn with a steady flame. With practise they become accomplished lovers who are as eager to satisfy their partners as themselves.

Sexual match: Scorpio, Cancer.

Sexual preferences: Any slow lovemaking position appeals to the Taurean, including petting and foreplay (especially oral sex), side–by–side and "spoons".

GEMINI (*22 May – 21 June*)

Sexual profile: As contrary as a summer breeze, those born under this air sign are restless, versatile, unexpected and inventive. Highly sexed Geminis are connoisseurs of the art of love. They need variety to keep them satisfied, but only within their comfort zone. Expect a Gemini to be eager to try new ideas, no matter how outrageous – but only in the privacy of the bedroom.

Sexual match: Pisces, Leo.

Sexual preferences: Role play, fun and games and any sexual positions not tried before.

CANCER (*21 June – 22 July*)

Sexual profile: As this is a water sign expect Cancerians to be soft, sensitive and emotional types driven by powerful hidden forces like a spring tide. They feel things deeply – physically and emotionally – and need the security of a strong emotional bond. They'll never enjoy sex for its own sake but show great passion with a caring partner.

Sexual match: Libra, Taurus.

Sexual preferences: Petting and foreplay and positions that allow for sensual lovemaking such as side-by-side and "spoons".

LEO (*23 July – 23 August*)

Sexual profile: The typical Leo is a real animal between the sheets. This is a fire sign so little wonder Leos are demanding, dominating, tempestuous and passionate. They have great sexual stamina and would spend all day making love if they could. But Leos are easily embarrassed, so don't expect anything too off-the-wall.

Sexual match: Capricorn, Gemini.

Sexual preferences: No-nonsense foreplay followed by dominant man-on-top or woman-on-top positions – with a little bondage, providing they do the tying up.

VIRGO (*24 August – 22 September*)

Sexual profile: Virgoans – as befits an earth sign – can be very "earthy" indeed. The typical Virgo dares to be different and so anything naughty, adventurous, risqué, daring and spontaneous attracts someone born under this sign. Reticent by nature they need a confident and impulsive lover to take the lead and bring out the best (or worst!) in them.

Sexual match: Sagittarius, Aquarius.

Sexual preferences: Standing sex, al fresco sex, sex on the kitchen table, role play (especially bondage).

LIBRA (*23 September – 23 October*)
Sexual profile: Libra lovers are romantics and, unsurprisingly for an air sign, have their head in the clouds. Anything intimate, cosy and tender appeals to their loving natures, such as candle-lit suppers followed by a cuddle on the hearthrug. They like to experiment but don't expect them to suggest anything too outrageous.
Sexual match: Cancer, Sagittarius.
Sexual preferences: Petting and kissing and any position that offers lots of skin-to-skin contact whether man on top, woman on top or side by side.

SCORPIO (*24 October – 22 November*)
Sexual profile: A typical Scorpio is intense, temperamental, passionate, powerful and moody at the best of times – let alone in bed. Scorpio is a water sign, so when it comes to sexual frolics imagine a mighty ocean that suddenly whips up a storm of passion.
Sexual match: Taurus, Pisces.
Sexual preferences: Oral sex, dominant positions such as man- or woman-on-top and power play such as bondage and chastisement – but only if they're in charge.

 **SAGITTARIUS** (*23 November – 21 December*)
Sexual profile: This is a fire sign and Sagittarians certainly make hot lovers. They are totally candid about their sexual likes and dislikes and also very enthusiastic and playful with the right partner. They are adventurous in the bedroom and ever eager to experiment. Don't expect to get much sleep when a Sagittarian is in the mood for love.
Sexual match: Virgo, Libra.
Sexual preferences: Spirited foreplay, fun and games, and sexual positions with lots of rolling and tumbling and high jinks.

 **CAPRICORN** (*22 December – 20 January*)
Sexual profile: This is an earth sign and, like a dormant volcano, Capricorn lovers can appear cool on the outside and yet smoulder inside, waiting for the right moment to erupt into passion. They're not greatly interested in experimentation, so don't expect surprises. But once aroused they'll last all night – the goat isn't a symbol of sex for nothing.
Sexual match: Leo, Scorpio.
Sexual preferences: Plenty of intimate foreplay and oral sex, and any variation on the man-on-top or woman-on-top themes.

AQUARIUS (*21 January – 18 February*)
Sexual profile: This is an air sign and, when it comes to bedroom antics, Aquarians are as capricious as the wind. They're extrovert lovers who'll enjoy anything new. They act like they've had a rush of blood to the head – and enjoy sex that way too.
Sexual match: Aries, Virgo.
Sexual preferences: Oral sex – especially soixante-neuf – and sex in the hall, on the stairs, in the car and the open air, in fact any position that offers a new and exciting experience.

PISCES (*19 February – 20 March*)
Sexual profile: Members of this water sign are dreamy and romantic, like a sun-kissed lake. Pisceans like to lie back and think of – well anything at all, really. So any ideas that let them express their imaginative side appeal to Pisceans, such as making love in the bath, on the beach or in the woods.
Sexual match: Gemini, Scorpio.
Sexual preferences: Romantic foreplay, spontaneous moments of passion, fantasy and role play and any sexual position that provides for imaginative lovemaking.

PETTING & FOREPLAY

1

*"Seduction is enticing someone
to do what they secretly
wanted to do already."*

Walter Rant

Like building a bonfire, explosive sex needs a slow, steady buildup until you reach the moment when you create the spark that sets your passion afire. This is why petting and foreplay are the ideal – indeed essential – preliminaries to sex. Women need these tender caresses to satisfy their emotional and physical needs. But men too benefit from loving sessions of petting and foreplay to get the most out of their lovemaking.

If your partner is fatigued or stressed after a hard and tiring day, he or she may not be feeling particularly sexy. But an experienced and understanding lover will soon change all that. With deft and artful movements of hand, lips and tongue, they will explore those secret and magical areas of their partner's body that they know can stir the embers of their arousal.

If you do not yet know your partner's body well enough to launch them on course for ecstasy with consummate ease then now is the time to find out. The following pages suggest ways to turn your partner's smouldering passion into a raging sexual inferno…

IN THE MOOD FOR LOVE...

The bonfire party is over. The guests have departed, leaving host and hostess alone – at last. Time to relax, but that needn't mean the fun and games are over for the night. Now is the time for fireworks of a different kind. The hostess is looking particularly gorgeous in that little black number she keeps for occasions like this. The host sidles up behind her, wrapping his arms around her waist and nuzzling her neck with delicate kisses.

As he feels her body begin to respond, he gently unfastens a few buttons on her dress and strokes her soft skin. Before long, gentle petting develops into a passionate embrace as their ardour slowly mounts...

For a satisfying and rewarding sex life that also strengthens the relationship it is important to keep the warm glow of romance alive through spontaneous moments of tenderness like this. The post-party mood is ideal; you're relaxed and contented, you've spent time looking good for your guests and so you know you'll look good to your partner too.

> *"Any piece of clothing can be sexy...*
> *with a quietly passionate woman inside it."*
> O Magazine

A man should never be in too much of a hurry to get his lover into bed. All females burn with a long fuse, so their partners need to take their time. The watchwords are tease and tantalize. Seek out areas of her body that you haven't explored before and see what effect it has. You might be surprised.

Neck and ears are particularly sensitive, but all parts of the female form respond to a tender touch. Caress her body through her clothes, letting your fingers glide over her curves. Her skin feels particularly sexy through a layer of soft silky material, so this is for your enjoyment too.

Now reach into her clothing to explore her smooth skin directly, loosening a few buttons, lowering a zip, raising the hem of her skirt slightly on your voyage of discovery. Don't rush to touch her most highly erotic – or *erogenous* – zones, though. She knows where you're heading and the sense of anticipation she is feeling is exquisite torture to her.

Stroke her sides in small, circular movements, slowly edging towards her breasts before changing course and heading downwards. Then, just as you are nearing that soft mound of flesh at the base of her abdomen, the pubic mound, take your teasing touch in another direction, and stroke her thighs. Delaying intimate contact in this way is highly arousing for a woman – as you'll discover in the way she responds.

Above The more delicate the caress, the more powerfully a woman's body will respond. Light kisses to her neck, combined with a strong hold at her waist, will make a woman feel both loved and secure.

Above Take your time to reveal your partner's body, removing each item of clothing slowly and in stages. Pause to kiss, stroke and admire the new areas of flesh as they are exposed.

Right Now it is the woman's turn to show what hands and lips can do. Slowly unbutton his shirt and reach inside to explore the contours of his body before planting the lightest of kisses on his chest.

Left Stay patient and keep your touch light and gentle, even as you begin to remove the last items of clothing. Always be aware of new areas to discover and relish.

Above A woman can also show how much she enjoys the sight of her partner's body. By taking her time to remove his clothes she will delay the action and make his sexual feelings soar.

Far Right Allow yourselves to sink slowly to the floor and enjoy the sumptuous feeling of two naked bodies intertwined and lost in passion.

> ## "Women need a reason to make love.
> ## Men just need a place."
> ### Billy Crystal

It can seem like sexual agony for a man, too, as he longs to enjoy her body to the full. But patience is a virtue that earns its own reward and a man will find his sexual enjoyment is greatly enhanced if he allows his own passion to build as slowly as his partner's.

By taking time to explore all of a woman's body, a man soon discovers just what kinds of sexual caress deliver the strongest arousal. An attentive lover will pay close attention to the way his partner reacts to his tender touch and uses these cues to guide his actions (see *A Woman's Signs of Passion,* right). All good things come to those who wait, including earth-shattering, orgasmic, explosive sex.

If hands can kindle the spark of passion that's nothing to what the mouth will do. While exploring your partner's body with your fingertips, kiss her lips and probe her mouth with your tongue. Follow this with delicate kisses around her face and neck. Don't stop there. Plant moist caresses across her breasts as though tracing an imaginary necklace.

Cup your lips around her nipples, sucking them and teasing them with your tongue. Once the nipples are moistened, blow across them — your breath will cause a slight chill that may send an erotic tingle through her body. Carry on down her abdomen (but not too far — yet) and inner thigh, tracing a line of kisses up, down and up again. Moisten her skin with your tongue and, again, blow across it to enhance the sensation.

EXPLOSIVE FACTS: A WOMAN'S SIGNS OF PASSION

All women vary widely in the way they respond sexually. Don't expect ear-splitting cries of passion. The powerful feelings she is experiencing may leave her speechless so look for less obvious signs. She may give a low groan, a soft gasp, or slight intake of breath. She may arch her back and tense her muscles. These signs all show you're on the right track so keep doing what you are doing, even to climax (see page 38). Then, once she relaxes you'll know her orgasm is over for now – but more may follow. Don't forget, women can enjoy multiple orgasms so the more ways you find to pleasure your partner the better.

SEXY AND ASSERTIVE…

If the man seems slow to act then this is a golden opportunity for a woman to take the initiative, beginning with whispered sultry, sexy words, and gentle fingertip touches. This is an example of being sexually assertive and can enhance his enjoyment as much as hers. Sexual assertiveness in a woman means taking responsibility for her own sexual wants and needs. It is a skill that blossoms with practise.

Try some seduction. Raise your dress slightly to reveal a little more thigh and climb onto his lap, wrapping your legs around him. By remaining clothed you conceal more than you reveal yet offer tempting glimpses of flesh – a powerful turn-on for a man. Make it clear you are controlling the pace and he must follow your lead. If this is a new experience for him he'll find it all the more exciting and arousing.

Many men do not grasp the full importance that women attach to petting. When a man is in charge these early caressing touches lead to intercourse far too soon. But petting has a special role for a woman. Periods of undemanding romantic contact prove to her that she is loved for herself and not regarded as a mere sex object.

By taking the initiative a woman can delay the moment when gentle petting becomes overtly sexual and ensures that all her needs are being met – emotional as well as physical. Take it slowly, this moment is about your enjoyment as much as his.

This is also the chance to discover hidden male erogenous zones of which your partner may be unaware. Stroke his ears, neck, arms and shoulders. Loosen buttons on his shirt to reach in and stroke his chest. A man's nipples are not as sensitive as a woman's but still respond to touch and can become erect when aroused. Caress his back, thighs and buttocks too, but avoid the more intimate areas unless you want to speed the session to full-on sex.

Left Top Actions speak louder than words, so if you are in the mood for love and your man hasn't responded show him how you feel by moving closer and planting a light kiss on his lips.

Left Centre Once he has got the message, you can sidle closer and slowly wrap one leg over his, while beginning to unfasten a few buttons to show him what he can expect.

Left Bottom There's no rush. If you are enjoying the sense of empowerment that comes from asserting your sexual self, make it clear you are going to take your time and that he will just have to be patient and wait.

Top Left Now you are ready to climb onto his lap and take command of the situation. Having loosened your own clothes, you can start to unfasten some of his buttons too.

Top Right You have him where you want him – lying helpless beneath you. Start to explore his body and let him begin to explore yours, but stay away from prime erogenous zones – for now, anyway.

Above For a woman, the emotional bond is as important as the physical experience, so make the most of your loving contact, with more tender kisses and caresses.

Left Now you can let your partner off the leash and allow him to enjoy himself by encouraging him to investigate all areas of your body. Where you go from here is completely up to you…

Above Let your partner explore you, looking for new places to touch and new ways to touch them. This will be an education for both of you if he manages to discover a "magic button" you didn't even know you had!

Now you're ready to get fully undressed, but don't be in too much of a hurry. Sexy stripping is arousing for both men and women. Men are visual creatures, turned on as much by the sight of a partner's body as the feel. Women are more tactile than visual but will enjoy looking at a smartly dressed male while stripping off themselves.

Slowly and sexily loosen buttons and zips and offer parts of your body to be kissed. Or undress each other, stroking and feeling each area of flesh that is exposed. Now think about other ways to make this moment last.

Encourage your partner to explore your body, and further his education. Direct his hand to where you like to be touched and – by word or subtle movement – indicate how hard or gently, how fast or slowly, you like to be stimulated. This way your lover lets your arousal grow steadily and does not target primary erogenous zones before you're ready.

If there are areas you don't like being touched – perhaps your ears or neck – find a subtle way to deflect your lover without spoiling the mood. Simply offering another part of you for him to caress will convey the message without causing offence.

Men also need to know what effect they are having so a woman shouldn't be shy about expressing her feelings. Press your body against his hand in response to his touch and tell him how much you are enjoying it.

You'll have found some erogenous zones by now, but keep exploring – there are plenty more. One neglected area is the perineum, the area at the top of the thighs between anus and genitals – in both sexes. It is highly arousing when stimulated by a partner's fingers or, better still, mouth and tongue. In men there is another area, too, that a woman may wish to visit (see *The Male G-spot*, below).

EXPLOSIVE FACTS: THE MALE G-SPOT

Having his perineum stimulated is highly arousing for a man, and not just because the skin here is sensitive. It is the external region closest to the prostate gland – an organ sometimes dubbed the "male G-spot". The prostate's main job is to produce some of the seminal fluid in the man's ejaculate, but it is a powerful sex organ in its own right. This walnut-sized organ at the base of the bladder can be stimulated more directly if a partner gently inserts her finger into the man's anus and rubs the front wall of the rectum. Applying a little lubrication to the finger makes this easier.

Below Men often know less about their own body than they do about a woman's. This is where a loving partner can help, by teaching her man what his own body is capable of experiencing.

MUTUAL MASTURBATION…

Stimulating the genitals by hand is called masturbation, whether on oneself or a partner. When men masturbate they are often over eager and ejaculate too soon. A loving partner can show him how it should be done. Having a woman fondle his penis is a huge turn-on for a man. The sensation may be too powerful, however, and if she's not careful he may climax too soon. This is a woman's chance to take control, to delay his orgasm until he begs for release (see *The Male Pleasure Zones*, below).

> *"Licence my roving hands and let them go, Behind, before, above, between, below."*
> John Donne

EXPLOSIVE FACTS: THE MALE PLEASURE ZONES

In its non-aroused (flaccid) state the penis hangs down limply. As a man gets aroused it hardens and lengthens. At the same time the sack-like scrotum encasing his testicles becomes tighter, smoother and more sensitive. The long shaft of the penis is capped by a dome-like head or glans, the most sensitive part. In uncircumcised men the glans is covered by a hood of skin, or foreskin, which roles back to form a collar. In circumcised men the glans is permanently exposed. On the underside of the penis, where glans and shaft meet, is an especially sensitive region called the frenulum. By handling his penis and testicles a woman soon discovers just how her partner likes to be stimulated.

MASTURBATING HIM…

To give your lover a powerful sexual experience begin by cupping and squeezing his testicles. Now encircle the shaft of the penis with thumb and fingers and slowly draw them up and down. Begin slowly and increase the pace until you have a steady rhythm.

Be guided by him on the amount of friction he likes but don't let him dictate the pace. If he gets too aroused too quickly then slow down and, if necessary, pause to let his erection subside slightly before increasing the rhythm and making him hard again.

Stimulating his penis close to the frenulum and glans enhances the sensation even more. If he is uncircumcised you can draw the foreskin back and forth over the glans. But the glans itself may be too sensitive to touch directly. If so he will tell you.

Gauge how close he is to climaxing and decide what your next move should be, it's your choice. If you decide to bring him to orgasm by hand then slow the pace as he begins to ejaculate but don't stop until he relaxes, when you will know he's spent. You might choose to stimulate him orally instead (see page 26).

Right As a woman you can find exciting new ways to masturbate your lover that he might not even have thought about himself. Be inventive in the way you stroke and fondle his penis – you'll know when you've got it right.

MASTURBATING HER…

The average man can usually locate his partner's vagina, if only to insert his penis, but may know less about the rest of her body. If so, it's high time to find out (see *The Female Pleasure Zones*, right).

As with stroking other parts of a woman's body slow, gentle, teasing touches are the most arousing. Female pleasure zones are so sensitive that being too direct or forceful is pointless. Be patient. Begin slowly and easily. Start by stroking the soft skin between thigh and outer labium, using long, slow, delicate fingertip touches. Run your fingers along the edge of the labia, again with long, slow movements. As your partner becomes aroused her labia will separate to let you explore the soft, moist, delicate region inside.

Notice how your partner responds to your touch. She may press against you if she needs more pressure, or hold your wrist if the sensation is too much to bear. If you keep your movements light and gentle you can run your fingertips along the inner labia and around the urethra (the U-spot) and the vaginal opening.

Your partner may need to show you exactly how and where she likes to be touched. She may tell you directly what she enjoys but otherwise let her sounds and movements reveal her feelings. Think of her as a finely tuned musical instrument and you are playing her with the deft touch of a virtuoso musician.

As her passion increases she'll become very moist around and inside the vagina and this will let you insert a finger to enhance her arousal. The middle finger is usually longest and allows you to use long strokes and rub different areas of the inner wall. Change the rhythm and pressure to vary the sensation but never be too rough.

If your partner is highly aroused you can insert both middle and index fingers. Hold your hand vertically to push them in and then turn it through ninety degrees, moving your fingers in and out. The stretching sensation she will experience can be highly pleasurable – but be guided by her. If two fingers are uncomfortable then revert to one.

Although women produce a natural lubricating fluid when aroused, how much varies from woman to woman. Without it, manual stimulation (and penetration) is painful. There are proprietary lubricants available from pharmacists or you can moisten your finger first with your mouth. Lack of lubrication is less of a problem with oral sex…

Left Fingertips are best for exploring a woman's more sensitive areas. Make a 'V' shape with your index and middle fingers and stroke them gently either side and along her labia. This should have an explosive effect.

ORAL SEX…

There is no more intimate act that a partner can perform than oral sex. The mouth and tongue make ideal pleasuring devices. The lips are soft and moist and deliver light and delicate kisses or firmer sucking pressure. The tongue can be soft or firm, giving gentle caresses and firm licks. Used imaginatively, the mouth can send a woman into orbit (or at the very least she'll see stars).

PLEASURING HIM…

Oral sex on a man is called fellatio. The benefits for him are obvious, but many women also enjoy this intimate contact. It can bring her emotionally closer to her lover and help her understand his sexual responses. She should only do it if she really wants to, though. No woman should feel coerced into performing oral sex (see *Don't Let Him Blackmail You*, left).

It is best to find a comfortable position for oral sex. For example, the man could recline on a sofa or sit back in an armchair while his partner kneels between his parted thighs. Start by kissing him along his inner thigh or the base of his belly, not quite touching his genitals, to build the suspense. Kiss and lick his scrotum, and maybe take one or both testicles in your mouth, then release them gently and blow over the now moistened skin.

To continue the buildup, lick along the shaft, from base to head, varying your movements from long, languid strokes to delicate dabbing touches. Use lips and tongue alternately to stimulate the frenulum, continuing for as long as your partner responds. When ready, take the head of the penis in your mouth and slowly lick it before applying sucking pressure. How much of the shaft you take in is up to you.

The glans and top of the shaft are by far the most sensitive areas so you don't have to draw too much into your mouth to provide powerful stimulation. By moving your head up and down you mimic your hand movements when masturbating him, stepping up the pace until he's close to climax. Some women are happy to have their partner ejaculate in their mouth, but for others it's taboo. It's a woman's choice (see *The First Swallow*, opposite).

EXPLOSIVE FACTS: DON'T LET HIM BLACKMAIL YOU

A woman shouldn't feel she "owes" her partner oral sex just because he performed it on her. Men enjoy pleasuring a woman in this way for its own sake – otherwise they wouldn't bother.

Right Oral pleasuring is the ultimate sexual turn-on for a man. There are many ways to vary the experience, including blowing gently across his moistened penis and even humming while it is in your mouth.

EXPLOSIVE FACTS: THE FIRST SWALLOW...

Your partner should tell you when he's about to ejaculate so you can decide whether to let him come in your mouth or bring him to climax with your hand. However, your partner may not know how close he actually is to orgasm or may be too aroused to speak, so look for other signs, such as a change in breathing and tension in the abdomen and thighs. A woman in a loving, monogamous relationship has little to fear from semen. She can decide whether to swallow or spit it out into a tissue. A loving partner shouldn't seek to coerce a woman into doing something she feels uncomfortable about.

PLEASURING HER…

Oral sex on a woman is called cunnilingus. Any position that comfortably grants a man access to his partner's vulva will do. He could lay his partner on the bed with her knees raised and parted while he sits on the edge of the bed with his head between her thighs.

All men should relish the sight and taste of this most intimate part of a woman and most would happily perform oral sex even if their partners didn't much care for the experience. Happily, few women pass up the chance to receive such close personal attention. Many women who have difficulty climaxing through penetrative sex experience their first and most powerful orgasms through oral sex.

Start by teasing and tantalizing your partner. Kiss her inner thigh and pubic mound, always approaching – but not quite reaching – the vulva itself. Kiss and lick the crease between her thigh and outer labium, then plant a firm, protracted kiss directly on the labia. Tug on one outer labium with your lips and then the other. Now repeat more gently with the highly sensitive inner labium.

You may need to raise her knees and spread her thighs wide to access all her sexual zones with ease. Take your time. Pause to enjoy

the sight of this "secret garden" and say how beautiful she is. Many women feel self-conscious about their body and need a man's reassurance that you find all parts of them sexy.

Use your tongue to lick, stroke and probe her contours and crevices, keeping your actions gentle – remember, this area is very sensitive. If your partner can stand it, suck her clitoris, or moisten it with your tongue and blow across it. You can be slightly more forceful with her vagina, pushing your tongue into her as far as you can go – having a long tongue is a definite advantage…

Your partner will become moist as her arousal soars, so savour the smell and taste of her. Each woman has her own unique sexual musk that is highly arousing to her man. You can make her climax using your mouth alone or add manual stimulation, stroking her perineum or the sides of her labia, or rubbing and squeezing the clitoris through its hood. Notice how she responds as you increase the pace and pressure until you find the ideal level of stimulation. Now that she's fully aroused you may both prefer to switch to penetrative sex. If so, which position should you adopt? Luckily there are lots to choose from, as you'll discover in *Chapter 2*…

Above When pleasuring a woman try to be as imaginative as possible, alternating between your lips, tongue and your whole mouth. Vary the pressure, and be aware of how she responds.

EXPLOSIVE SEX SEQUENCES

2

"Sex is emotion in motion."

Mae West

There are numerous positions that you and your partner can enjoy to add spice to your lovemaking and help you reach the heights of ecstasy together. Sexual variety is important, and not just to avoid boredom. Changing position ensures that you both receive the sexual stimulation you need. Studies show that when couples vary their positions regularly women are far more likely to experience orgasms through penetrative sex alone.

Including a range of positions in your lovemaking also allows you to vary the pace, slowing arousal for the man until his partner can catch up and – ideally – they climax together. Simultaneous orgasms are great, of course, but not essential. So long as you both feel satisfied then your intimacy will have achieved everything you could wish for.

Like a firework display, lovemaking starts slowly and builds to an earth-shaking climax, leaving you with a warm afterglow. The following sequences not only describe some of the many positions you can adopt during sex but also illustrate how you can move from one to the next seamlessly, like a beautifully choreographed ballet. Sex is the dance of love, but with a difference – like a firework display, it has a truly explosive finale!

SEQUENCE 1

Moving seamlessly from foreplay to intercourse without losing the romance is important if both partners are to stay in the mood for lovemaking. This sequence makes the transition smoothly – yet imaginatively…

▼ **1** This is a loving way to begin sex. The man sits in a relaxed pose on the bed while his partner climbs onto his lap and straddles him. They gaze into each other's eyes and kiss and caress. They can nuzzle and stroke each other's neck, back and shoulders. The man can feel his partner's breasts, and caress her thighs and vulva, before gently inserting a finger into her to stimulate her further and enhance her arousal.

• **EXPLOSIVE TIP:** *The couple should continue this gentle foreplay for as long as is pleasurable.*

EXPLOSIVE FACTS:
THE SEXUAL MIND

Men and women differ widely in what triggers their sexual arousal, how they like to be stimulated and the time it takes them to climax. For a man, erotic images may be enough to inflame his ardour. For a woman, mood, monthly cycle, and her feelings towards her partner are also important. Other factors, like stress or fatigue, affect both sexes. This is why it is vital to create the right mood for sex with plenty of petting and foreplay before moving on to intercourse. Couples should be aware of their partner's responses at all times and use eye contact and caresses to strengthen the emotional ties between them.

2 When the man judges his partner is fully aroused he places the head of his penis against her vagina, pulls her towards him and enters her. She can wrap her arms around his neck while he places his hands under her thighs and lifts her off the ground. The woman wraps her legs around his waist. Turning round, he carefully positions her over the bed, bending his knees, leaning forward and placing one hand on the bed for support to set her down gently while still keeping his penis inside her.

3 As the man leans forward, supporting his weight on his arms, his partner takes her arms from around his neck and lies back while unwrapping her legs from his waist. The man now increases the pace and depth of his thrusts, flattening himself or standing upright to change the angle of penetration. He can raise one or both of her legs to vary the direction of his thrusts even more to stimulate different parts of her vagina.

SEQUENCE 2

This sequence allows the woman to take the lead in love-making, pleasuring her partner orally and then choosing the moment when she wants to move on to penetrative sex while retaining a sense of control throughout.

▼ **I** This is a wonderfully liberating sequence for a woman who is already highly aroused through foreplay. She ensures her partner is sexually stimulated through oral sex and then chooses when to take their lovemaking to the next stage. The man sits on the edge of the bed supporting himself on his elbows, with thighs comfortably parted, so he is open to his partner's lips and tongue. She kneels before him and strokes his penis with long, languorous movements until he's fully erect, then takes the head of his penis in her mouth to stimulate him further, taking care not to over-arouse him before she's ready.

• **EXPLOSIVE TIP:** *The man needs to ensure his partner remains fully aroused, by stroking and squeezing her breasts, for example — or he may find he's closer to climaxing than she is.*

▲ **2** When ready, the woman climbs onto her partner's lap and lowers herself onto his penis, deciding for herself how deeply she wants to be penetrated. By using rocking movements of her hips she can control the pace and depth of the penetration, twisting her pelvis slightly to change the angle. If she wants greater control she can lean forward and place both knees on the edge of the bed. This is a very loving position as the couple can look into each other's eyes, kiss and caress to strengthen the emotional bond.

• **EXPLOSIVE TIP:** *As the woman is doing most of the work here, her partner's hands are free to squeeze and fondle her breasts, stroke her thighs, and reach behind to caress her back and bottom.*

EXPLOSIVE FACTS:
STAGES OF MALE
AROUSAL

Sexual arousal in a man begins with the *excitement* phase, when his penis lengthens and hardens. As his arousal grows he enters the second, *plateau*, phase – usually much shorter in men than women – and may ejaculate too soon unless careful. An experienced lover learns to extend the plateau phase until his partner is sexually satisfied (see page 56). At the end of this phase there's a period of *ejaculatory inevitability* when a man can't stop himself ejaculating. During the third phase, *orgasm and ejaculation*, semen (sperm and seminal fluid) is released in a series of rhythmic spurts. This is followed by *resolution* and relaxation. Unlike a woman it may be many minutes, hours or longer before a man can be aroused again. Once aroused he'll find it easier to extend his *plateau* phase to bring his partner to orgasm. After orgasm he may find it hard to keep awake, a potential cause of discord as women often want to kiss, cuddle and talk afterwards.

◀ **3** The woman gently pushes her partner back so she's in full control, in the classic woman-on-top position (see page 54) and can raise or lower her hips, or rock back and forth to control the pace of the action. There's little for the man to do in this position, a novel experience for him perhaps, other than caress his partner's breasts and thighs. They can maintain eye contact throughout, fully expressing their depth of feeling for each other.

• **EXPLOSIVE TIP:** *This is an ideal sequence to use when a man has already climaxed once as it is easier for his partner to stimulate his erection again. As a man usually takes much longer to ejaculate the second time, it gives his partner more time to reach her own climax.*

▼ **4** The woman now leans forwards or backwards to change the angle so that her partner's penis is stimulating the most sensitive areas of her vagina. In this way she can maintain a steady pace to extend their lovemaking until she's close to climaxing and can also squeeze her pelvic floor muscles around her partner's penis (see page 53) to provide extra stimulation for him and ensure he does not lose his erection.

• **EXPLOSIVE TIP:** *In this position the woman may be better placed than her partner to reach down to rub her vulva for extra stimulation, if necessary, to help bring herself to climax.*

EXPLOSIVE FACTS: SEXY CONDOM CAPERS

If couples are using condoms for barrier contraception they must ensure that the condom is in place before intercourse as there's a risk that some "pre-ejaculate" may emerge before they are ready. Also known as "pre-come", pre-ejaculate contains sperm and can be released before full ejaculation occurs. To avoid spoiling the sexual mood, the woman can fit the condom on the man herself, making it a novel part of their foreplay, using lots of teasing touches as she places the sheath on the head of the penis and then slowly strokes it into position – taking as long as she likes to do so…

SEQUENCE 3

This time the man is in control, using his mouth to arouse his partner, always looking to gauge her response to his oral stimulation so he will know when the time is right to switch to penetrative sex.

▼ **I** The woman sits on the edge of the bed with her partner kneeling between her thighs, caressing her vulva with his lips. He then uses his tongue, varying the action from gentle laps to strong thrusting movements that penetrate her vagina. The woman may lean back or lie flat, passively enjoying the stimulation, or lean forward to engage with her partner by stroking his head and neck and whispering sexy words in his ear.

• **EXPLOSIVE TIP:** *By resting one or both feet on her partner's back a woman comfortably spreads her thighs very wide, allowing his mouth full access.*

EXPLOSIVE FACTS: FEMALE SEXUAL AROUSAL

In a woman, sexual arousal begins with the *excitement* phase when her nipples harden and become erect and her areolae (pigmented areas surrounding the nipples) darken. Her vagina releases lubricating fluid, and the clitoris grows erect. With continued stimulation the woman enters the second, *plateau*, phase, when her vagina lengthens and widens. This phase may last many minutes – much longer than in a man – until further stimulation "tips her over the edge" into *orgasm*, which is the third phase. During the final *resolution* phase she relaxes, feeling a deep sense of contentment, and may want to cuddle and talk to strengthen the bond in the relationship and her own sense of feeling valued. Unlike a man, women are easily re-aroused at this stage, and have the potential for multiple orgasms (see page 86).

▶ **2** As the woman grows aroused her partner stands up slowly, placing his hands under her thighs to raise her legs and lower her onto her back. He enters her and begins slow thrusting movements. From a standing position he can control the pace and depth of his thrusts and raise or lower her legs to vary the angle of penetration.

• **EXPLOSIVE TIP:** *If the woman wants to play a more active part she can rock her hips in synchrony with her partner's thrusting movements.*

▼ **3** He now leans over her, supporting his body on his outstretched arms, or raises his partner's legs higher, resting her ankles on his shoulders. The man can now thrust into his partner very deeply, a dominant position many women find arousing. He should avoid causing discomfort or pain, however. By watching his partner closely he can vary the depth and pace to match her responses. The woman can wrap her legs around him to pull him closer.

SEQUENCE 4

Mutual oral sex is pleasurable for both partners but men and women have different arousal times and a man may climax too soon. This sequence helps to delay a man's responses to match those of his partner.

▲ **I** The woman lies on her back with legs comfortably parted and knees slightly raised. The man climbs over her and adopts the "69 position", placing his thighs either side of her head. He lowers himself until his penis and testicles are accessible to her mouth while placing his own mouth on her vulva. If the woman supports his hips she can stop him pressing down too far. While he stimulates her with his tongue, she does the same to his testicles, but not his penis – for the moment.

• **EXPLOSIVE TIP:** *In this position the woman can kiss and lick her partner's perineum, arousing him without risking bringing him to a premature climax.*

> ### EXPLOSIVE FACTS: THE SQUEEZE TECHNIQUE
>
> For men who find it difficult to delay ejaculation long enough to satisfy their partner, the squeeze technique offers a solution. Here the man withdraws his penis from his partner's vagina and he (or she) squeezes the penis just below the head (glans) until his erection starts to subside. The man then resumes intercourse. This is repeated several times until his partner is close to climaxing. He then continues without interruption.

▲ **2** The couple roll onto their sides and the man draws his upper leg back and pushes his lower leg forward so his partner can use his inner thigh as a pillow. She does the same so his face rests on her thigh. Her vulva is now accessible to his mouth and tongue, and his penis is ideally placed for her. The woman now has more freedom of movement to perform fellatio, but still keeps the level of stimulation to a minimum.

• **EXPLOSIVE TIP:** *This relaxed and loving position can be maintained for as long as they like.*

▼ **3** As the couple approach orgasm they roll over again so she is now on top, a better position for her, allowing her to control the pace. The man continues to lick her vulva and she can push her groin onto his face to increase the stimulation. She performs oral sex on him, teasing him to delay his orgasm. This form of "girl power" is arousing for a woman and a novel experience for a man, making his own climax more powerful.

SEQUENCE 5

The man-on-top or "missionary" position is the most popular one for penetrative sex. But there are many variations to this classic pose that provide additional benefits and novelty for both partners.

▼ **1** The man lies on top of his partner, between her parted thighs, to enter her. Supported on hands/elbows and toes he moves his pelvis in a piston action to thrust in and out. Many women enjoy the submissive nature of this position, as the man is in control. For a more active role, the woman presses against the bed, to move her pelvis in time with his thrusts, and angles her body to direct his penis to the most sensitive areas of her vagina.

• **EXPLOSIVE TIP:** *By wrapping her legs around her partner's thighs and locking her ankles a woman can pull the man closer to her, and rub her groin against his to stimulate her clitoris.*

▲ **2** The man can grip his partner's legs to spread her thighs further apart. Now more of her vulva is stimulated by his thrusts, enhancing the sensation she experiences. The man can also direct the head of his penis more precisely to the front wall of her vagina, where the highly erogenous G-spot is located (see page 46).

• **EXPLOSIVE TIP:** *In a widely spread position it is easier for the woman to reach down and rub her clitoris. Watching her do this is a powerful turn-on for her partner.*

▼ **3** The man can also lift his partner's ankles above his shoulders and press them closer together to narrow the vaginal opening and increase the stimulation. He can swing his partner's legs from one side to the other – or flatten them against her chest, if she's supple enough. This allows him to change the angle of penetration and use shorter, faster strokes to bring her to climax.

• **EXPLOSIVE TIP:** *From this position the man can turn his partner over and penetrate her from behind – called rear-entry sex (see pages 70–73).*

SEQUENCE 6

Not all women find it easy to climax through vaginal stimulation alone. The following sequence incorporates a unique "coital alignment technique" (the "CAT") that stimulates the clitoris during intercourse.

▼ **1** In this sequence the man lies between his partner's legs, supporting himself on his hands. The woman's knees are raised and her feet flat on the bed. This allows the couple to maintain loving eye contact, and to kiss and caress each other. As in the previous sequence, a woman can play a more active role by moving her pelvis to complement her partner's thrusts. The woman's hands are free to run her fingers through her partner's hair, over his neck and back and down to his buttocks.

EXPLOSIVE FACTS: COITAL ALIGNMENT TECHNIQUE

A problem with penetrative vaginal intercourse is that it does not allow the penis to stimulate the clitoris, the most erotically sensitive part of a woman's body. The coital alignment technique or "CAT" is one solution. Here the couple position themselves so the base of the man's penis and pubic bone (part of his pelvis) rub against the woman's clitoris. The couple use synchronized back and forth or side-to-side rocking motions to increase the stimulation, helping the woman to climax. This technique can be used in both man- and woman-on-top positions.

▲ **2** Now the woman wraps her legs around her partner's waist and crosses her ankles to lock them in position and pull him closer. She can also put her arms around him and hug him. As well as being a loving gesture this will restrict her partner's movements slightly, allowing her to slow the pace of their lovemaking until her own slower sexual responses catch up with his.

• **EXPLOSIVE TIP:** *By sliding one of her hands between them down to the man's groin the woman can squeeze and stroke her partner's scrotum to help maintain his erection.*

▼ **3** Now the man lifts onto his knees and leans forward, supporting himself with his arms, to enter his partner from a higher angle. The woman still keeps her legs tightly wrapped around him to keep them close. The couple now use a rocking motion to continue their lovemaking (see *Coital Alignment Technique*, below left), so that the man's groin rubs against his partner's clitoris while his penis penetrates her vagina.

• **EXPLOSIVE TIP:** *Women who use this technique find they are more likely to climax through penetrative sex alone.*

SEQUENCE 7

Here's another approach to the man-on-top theme, providing a more dominant role for the male that both men and women can find equally arousing. It allows more variation in depth and angle of penetration.

▼ **I** This sequence starts with the classic man-on-top position, with the man between his partner's thighs and using rhythmic thrusts of his pelvis to stimulate her. Initially, the woman can move her pelvis in time with her partner but in later steps she may find her freedom of movement too restricted for this. As this sequence allows a couple to extend their lovemaking for far longer than the previous man-on-top positions, the man will need to delay his climax if his partner is to be satisfied and reach orgasm herself. Therefore these moves may be best reserved for times when a man has already ejaculated once, and the couple are enjoying another lovemaking session a little time afterwards, as he'll take longer to climax the second time.

EXPLOSIVE FACTS: THE G-SPOT

The most sexually sensitive area of the vagina is named the G-spot after German-American gynaecologist Dr Ernst Gräfenberg who first identified it. It is located on the front inner wall, about 5 cm (2 in) from the vaginal opening. During sex it swells slightly and may be felt as a bean-sized lump. It's packed with nerve endings that respond strongly to rhythmical rubbing and, more importantly, are connected to multiple nerve pathways that link the G-spot to key pleasure centres in the brain. Any sexual position and angle that puts the head of the penis in contact with the G-spot may bring a woman to orgasm. The G-spot can also be stimulated by the man during foreplay using his finger or a sex toy.

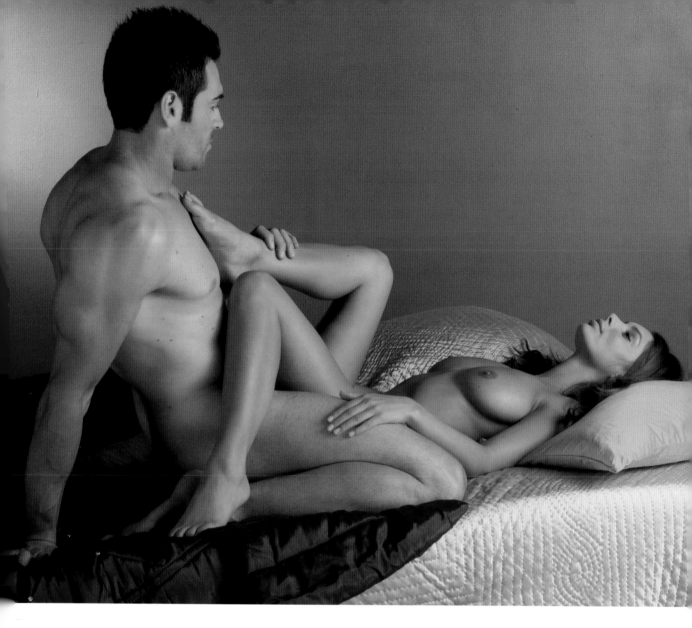

▲ **2** Now the man gathers his partner's legs by her calves or ankles and lifts them while raising himself into a kneeling position, spreading his partner's legs wide or pressing them together to narrow her vaginal opening and so increase the friction. From this position the man has a wide variety of angles to choose from. By leaning back further he can direct the head of his penis more precisely against the front inner wall of her vagina where the G-spot is located (see *The G-spot*, opposite). Or he can spread her legs wide and lean forwards to maintain a deeper thrusting movement that stimulates a region in the vagina called the A-spot (see *The A-spot*, page 49). He can also swing both of her legs to the side so that other parts of her vagina receive attention.

• **EXPLOSIVE TIP:** *The man should maintain eye contact with his partner throughout so the woman does not feel like a sex object and she should make it clear what she does — and doesn't — enjoy.*

"I think that sex is the best form of exercise."
Cary Grant

◄ 3 Still gripping her ankles or calves, the man folds his partner's legs back and places her feet against his chest. The woman can spread her knees to position them either side of her chest – if she's supple enough – while keeping her feet against him. The man continues with rapid thrusting movements or slows the pace if he's approaching his own climax too soon. The woman's freedom of movement is still limited but she can press her arms against the bed to lift her bottom and rock her pelvis.

• EXPLOSIVE TIP: *In this position it may be possible for the couple to use the rocking movement of the coital alignment technique (see page 44) to stimulate the woman's clitoris.*

▼ 4 Now the man crosses his partner's legs and gently pushes them down so her thighs press towards her chest. He must be careful not to press too far in this position as it may restrict his partner's breathing. She can guard against this by gripping his upper arms or shoulders to stop him pressing down too hard. The man now resumes his thrusting movements, making them shallow and rapid, to stimulate the front wall of her vagina, or pushes further in more slowly, to stimulate deeper regions, until both partners are near to peak arousal. He then holds back until his partner has climaxed and an experienced lover may be able to time his orgasm to coincide with hers (see page 56).

EXPLOSIVE FACTS: THE A-SPOT

There is a highly erotic zone deep inside the vagina that some experts claim rivals the G-spot in sensitivity. It is called the A-spot because it is located in a region of the vagina called the anterior fornix. Like the G-spot, the A-spot is located on the front inner wall of the vagina, but much further in – close to the cervix (the neck of the uterus). Because of its location the A-spot is easiest to reach by adopting sex positions that allow for deep entry. When men switch between shallow and deep penetration in this way – stimulating the two regions alternately – many woman find they can enjoy regular, powerful orgasms through penetrative sex alone.

SEQUENCE 8

If a man and woman both feel they're contributing equally to lovemaking then sexual intercourse becomes more of a partnership. The following sequence allows couples to take turns to control the action…

▲ **1** This sequence starts with the woman lying on her back with her legs apart but flat on the bed and the man lying between her thighs. The couple can stay in this position, kissing and caressing and maintaining loving eye contact, while the man uses rhythmic thrusting movements of his pelvis, maintaining a steady pace. When he decides that he wants to slow the pace, the man places his left leg outside his partner's right leg – while still keeping his right leg between her legs – and rolls into a side-by-side position. By keeping one hand behind his partner's back as he does this, he can guide her to roll at the same time so they move in sequence like dancers, without interrupting the lovemaking.

▶ **2** In this side-by-side position, the woman raises her upper leg and wraps it over her partner's waist while he places his upper leg over her lower thigh. As movement is more restricted like this, they can slow the pace right down, using gentle rocking movements to maintain sexual stimulation without the man climaxing too soon. In this position they can kiss and caress. Each one can stroke their partner's back, buttocks and thighs using slow, gentle, loving caresses and touches.

EXPLOSIVE FACTS: STRENGTHENING THE "LOVE MUSCLES"

The pelvic floor is a collection of muscles, ligaments and other structures that support the internal sex organs, bladder and rectum in both men and women. It is the pelvic floor muscles that you tighten to stop yourself urinating until you can find a toilet. These muscles play an important role in sex, too, hence their other name – the "love muscles". By contracting her pelvic floor muscles a woman can squeeze her vagina around her partner's penis during sex to provide additional stimulation for them both and also hold him inside her when they change position. A man can tighten his pelvic floor to delay ejaculation until his partner is close to orgasm. To make sure your pelvic floor muscles are fully toned and ready for enthusiastic bouts of lovemaking, you should exercise them regularly. Simply pretend that you're trying to stop yourself urinating (when you don't actually need to). Tighten them for a count of ten and then relax. Do this five times a day or so at discreet moments – and especially during sex.

▲ **3** Now the woman takes the initiative by pushing her partner's right shoulder back so he is lying supine and she is astride his waist. She is now ideally placed to take control, either by keeping her body flat on top of his and rocking steadily backwards and forwards with her pelvis to increase the pace of the stimulation, or by straightening her back so she is riding her partner, raising and lowering her pelvis to "pump" his penis in and out of her. She can provide additional stimulation by alternately tightening and relaxing her pelvic floor muscles (see *Strengthening the "Love Muscles"* on page 51) so that her vagina grips his penis in a "milking" action.

• **EXPLOSIVE TIP:** *The man's movement is a little restricted in this position but he need not remain totally passive. His partner's breasts are ideally placed to receive his attention, or he could reach round and stroke her thighs and buttocks.*

▲ **4** To slow the action again, the couple move into the side-by-side position once more, this time rolling to the other side. For extra variety, the woman wraps her legs around her partner's waist or places her legs between his. Again, couples can remain in this side-by-side position to enjoy the sense of togetherness it brings and so strengthen the emotional bond between them. Many women love the sense of "oneness" that such moments bring to their lovemaking. When both partners feel they are nearing the peak of their sexual arousal they can move into the man- or woman-on-top positions and step up the pace once again until they climax.

• **EXPLOSIVE TIP:** *It can be highly arousing – and fun! – to keep switching positions, rolling back into side-by-side and then into man-on-top or woman-on-top positions repeatedly.*

SEQUENCE 9

With the man held "captive' between his partner's legs, the on-top position allows a woman total control over the way she is sexually stimulated and especially in the pace, depth and angle of penetration.

▲ **I** The man lies on his back while his partner straddles his waist. She leans forward to direct his penis towards the sensitive front wall of her vagina, supporting her upper body on her hands. By rocking on her knees she "pumps" his penis. From his supine position the man enjoys the sight of her body as she uses him as a sex toy. He needn't be passive as his hands are free to caress his partner's sides and thighs and squeeze her breasts, now highly accessible.

◄ **2** For a change of pace and angle, the woman moves her legs in front of her and rests them on her lover's chest or shoulders. She can place her hands on either side of her for support and rock back and forth. A man doesn't receive so much stimulation in this situation so his partner could tighten her pelvic muscles rhythmically to squeeze his penis and help maintain his erection. In this way she extends their lovemaking, delaying his climax until she is close to hers.

• **EXPLOSIVE TIP:** *To help his partner keep her balance the man can reach forward to support her hips or waist or wrap his arms around her thighs.*

▼ **3** Placing her arms further back for support, the woman leans back so her partner's penis is rubbing more effectively against her G-spot. She'll be able to vary between a rocking and a pumping movement, supported by feet and arms. She must take care not to lean back too far as she is bending his erection away from its normal angle. So the man may prefer to lift his upper body, supporting himself on his arms, so his erection is at a more natural angle. He can then rock his pelvis in time with her movements to increase the stimulus and also free up a hand to stroke his partner's body.

EXPLOSIVE FACTS: THE U-SPOT

All parts of a woman's vulva are extremely sensitive, especially the clitoris. But there is another neglected region that produces a powerful erotic charge when stimulated by a man's fingers or tongue. This is the U-spot, an area of delicate flesh between the clitoris and the vagina that surrounds the opening to the urethra (the tube that carries urine out of the body). It is most easily stimulated orally or manually by the man during foreplay, or manually during rear-entry sex or by the woman herself in a woman-on-top position.

SEQUENCE 10

The woman-on-top position allows for adventurous activities and a range of novel sexual stimuli and can help a couple to regulate their responses and so climax together. Be warned – the following sequence is not for the fainthearted!

▶ **1** In this sequence the man lies on his back with his legs together while his partner climbs on top and straddles his waist, carefully lowering herself onto his erect penis. She then lies forward on top of him and stretches her legs out behind. If she places her hands on the bed on either side and keeps a foot on either side of her partner's legs she can push against the bed with her toes to provide the traction she needs to rock back and forth. As movement is relatively restricted here, this position allows for slow languorous lovemaking, providing enough stimulus to maintain his erection. She can also help him stay erect by squeezing her pelvic floor muscles to tighten her vagina around his penis.

▶ **2** Now the woman turns her body through ninety degrees by "walking" herself round using her hands and feet. Her partner can support her as she does this. This is easier if the woman is already highly aroused at this stage and her vagina is well lubricated so that it swivels around his penis easily. It is also important that the woman loosens the "grip" of her pelvic floor muscles on her partner's penis. She is now lying across her partner and if seen from above their bodies would form an X shape. In this position she can pause to raise and lower herself on her partner's penis, pushing up from her feet and hands, and also twist her body slightly to change the angle of entry. In this unique position both partners may discover sexual sensations not experienced before.

EXPLOSIVE FACTS: SIMULTANEOUS ORGASM

When a couple are sexually "in tune" they can time their arousal so that both climax together during penetrative sex in a "simultaneous orgasm". If couples can't achieve this through intercourse it doesn't mean their lovemaking is inferior or that there are problems with the relationship. Many couples enjoy satisfying sex simply by taking care to ensure that the woman has at least one orgasm (or preferably more!) before her partner climaxes. However, continued stimulation by his penis (or hands or mouth) may allow her to become aroused again (see page 86) so that she has another orgasm, this time coinciding with his. The best way to achieve a simultaneous orgasm is for the man to ensure his partner is nearing the peak of her sexual arousal, through oral and/or manual stimulation, for example, before he enters her. If he ensures his partner is close to orgasm (if necessary, with more manual stimulation) by the time he begins the rapid thrusting movements that are most likely to bring on his own orgasm, his partner may well climax at the same time as him.

◀ **3** The woman continues her circular movement, again using her hands and feet, until she is facing in the opposite direction. She raises herself onto her knees so she is sitting astride her partner once more, but facing in the opposite direction. She now places her feet under her so she is squatting over her man. In this position she can raise and lower her pelvis in a pumping action – the equivalent of the male's thrusting movement – and either continue until she climaxes or changes position again.

• **EXPLOSIVE TIP:** *The man enjoys this position because of the intimate view it affords of his partner's bottom. His hands are also free to stroke and squeeze her buttocks.*

▼ **4** From the previous woman-on-top position she can alter the angle of penetration again by pushing her legs back and leaning forward – taking care not to bend her partner's penis too far – or lie back and stretch out on her partner. By rocking her pelvis backwards and forwards the woman can continue to work her partner's penis inside her. Movement is very restricted in this position – especially for the man – and so it offers an ideal opportunity to slow the pace once again and hence extend lovemaking. The woman can rub her pubic mound and clitoris to help bring herself to orgasm.

• **EXPLOSIVE TIP:** *With his partner lying flat on top of him, the man can reach round to squeeze her breasts or stroke her thighs and pubic mound and, especially, her clitoris and U-spot to provide the extra stimulation she may need to climax simultaneously with him.*

! EXPLOSIVE WARNING ¡

The erect penis may seem to be a very sturdy organ during lovemaking but it is only flesh and blood, made firm by hydraulic pressure in the blood vessels. It can be damaged during adventurous sex and so a woman should take extra care – especially when changing position with her partner's penis still inside her – that she does not bend it too far.

SEQUENCE 11

The female-dominant position offers many other exciting ways for a woman to stimulate her partner and enjoy new sensations of her own. The couple can then switch to a side-by-side position to slow the pace.

▼ **1** With the man lying on his back his partner climbs astride him and lowers herself onto his penis. She can begin by raising and lowering her pelvis to "pump" his penis. She then brings her legs forward and places her feet towards her partner's shoulders. By leaning forwards and using a rocking back-and-forth motion she can rub her clitoris against his groin to vary the stimulation. The man can move his pelvis in rhythm with her and also stroke his partner's thighs and feel her breasts.

EXPLOSIVE FACTS: GOOD VIBRATIONS

The skin houses many types of nerve ending, each one responding to slightly different forms of sensation. Nerve endings in the penis and vagina react best to a rhythmic rubbing, but the ideal rhythm to trigger orgasm will vary from person to person and even from week to week in the same person. Long, slow rubbing movements may be best during the early arousal stages of sex, followed by a rapid, shallow action as the couple near climax. The best way to find out what works is through experiment – and practise.

▲ **2** When the man wants to be more active or his partner wants a rest they roll over into the side-by-side position, with the woman's feet on the man's shoulders or around his waist. Now he can begin more forceful thrusting movements, using his lower leg and lower shoulder and arm for leverage. If she prefers, the woman can now let her partner do all the work.

• **EXPLOSIVE TIP:** *The couple can remain locked together like this for as long as they like and continue until they climax or move on to the next position.*

▲ **3** Now the man turns his partner onto her back, with her feet against his shoulders, and takes the dominant man-on-top position. The man can keep his partner's legs pressed back against her, or part them so that her calves are either side of his head. By moving her legs up or down or to one side he can change the depth and angle of penetration to vary the stimulation she is receiving.

• **EXPLOSIVE TIP:** *The man can stay in this position until they both climax or – as before – they can change position again – the options are endless!*

SEQUENCE 12

The side-by-side position lends itself to relaxed, unhurried
lovemaking but there are ways to slow the pace down even
more and create a unique lovemaking experience.

▼ **1** If a woman wishes to take the initiative and assert her dominance
over her man – perhaps an experience that is as novel and exciting for
him as it is for her – then this is a sequence to try. The move starts with
the man on his back, waiting to find out what his partner is going to do.
She climbs on top and straddles his waist, lowering herself onto his erect
penis. She can either use the squatting position, supported on her feet, or
kneel with her legs on either side of him, to "pump" his penis in and out
of her. She can vary the sensation by rocking or gyrating her pelvis at the
same time and also using her pelvic "love muscles" (see page 51) to
squeeze and "milk" his penis.

• **EXPLOSIVE TIP:** *Because his partner is doing all the work here, the
man is free to concentrate on giving her extra pleasure by squeezing and
stroking all the parts of her body that he can reach.*

▲ **2** Now the woman can lean forward and push her legs back so that they are straight behind her and she is lying full out balanced on top of her lover. This position gives great skin-to-skin contact, with her pelvic mound and clitoral area pressed against his groin and her breasts pressed against his chest. Placing her arms on his shoulders she can rock back and forth to continue the pumping action and enjoy the increased sexual stimulation this provides for her. The couple can kiss and caress each other and the man can reach round to stroke his partner's back and buttocks at the same time.

▲ **3** The woman can use the grip she has on her partner's shoulders to steer him as they both roll over into the side-by-side position. If the couple now synchronize their pelvic movements they can produce a slow but powerful thrusting action that rhythmically drives his penis in and out of her vagina. If it is easier, the woman could place her upper leg over her partner's legs and the man can bring his upper leg forward so that he is less restricted and can use more powerful pelvic thrusts. They can continue this move to help enhance their state of arousal before moving on to the next step.

▶ **4** Now the woman places her two legs between her partners legs – a reversal of the "missionary position" – to give a completely new experience. This tightens her vagina around his penis to increase the friction and hence the stimulation they both receive as his erection rubs firmly against the inner wall of her vagina. Both partners can bring their knees forward and lean back to change the angle and vary the areas of the vagina that are being stimulated. In this position it is difficult for the man to use deeper and more powerful thrusting movements, which is of benefit to his partner as it slows his arousal time and extends their lovemaking so that both partners can enjoy the sensation for longer. He is still able to stimulate the sensitive areas of her vagina located close to the vaginal opening.

• **EXPLOSIVE TIP:** *It is important that men and women try to maintain loving eye contact and/or kiss and caress to strengthen their emotional ties during complex lovemaking positions like this.*

EXPLOSIVE FACTS: SEXUAL LUBRICATION

Glands inside the vagina and around the vaginal entrance produce a special lubricating fluid that makes penetrative sex more enjoyable and avoids painful rubbing and soreness. This fluid starts to flow as soon as a woman becomes sexually aroused, so it is vital that a man ensures his partner receives plenty of sexual stimulation, by hand or mouth, before attempting penetration. In some women the amount of fluid produced is insufficient for protracted periods of sex, especially if lovemaking is over-enthusiastic or prolonged. Saliva provides a handy alternative but there is a range of effective artificial lubricants available from pharmacies. Avoid petroleum-based types if using barrier contraception as they can damage the latex that condoms are made from.

SEQUENCE 13

Positions that restrict entry to the vagina also increase the friction and stimulation lovers experience. When combined with a side-by-side position, where movement is limited, this both enhances and extends lovemaking.

EXPLOSIVE FACTS: DELAYING A MAN'S ORGASM

If a man climaxes before he wants to and, especially, before his partner has been sexually satisfied, it is called premature ejaculation. It could be due to over-excitement or may simply be a "bad habit" learned in puberty. When boys first begin to masturbate they are in a hurry to climax – perhaps through misplaced sense of guilt or fear of discovery. If they never learn to hold back then premature ejaculation becomes habitual. Positions such as side-by-side that restrict a man's thrusting movements help to delay ejaculation. A man can also strengthen his pelvic floor muscles (see page 51) to help resist the urge to climax. The squeeze technique (see page 40), taught by relationship counsellors and sex therapists, is also of benefit. Men may find that having ejaculated once, through mutual masturbation, oral sex or penetrative sex, they can be re-aroused and continue lovemaking and then will take longer to climax the second time.

◀ **1** This sequence starts with the woman lying flat on top of her man with her legs behind her. This offers lots of skin-to-skin contact and the man can reach round to stroke his partner's back, buttocks and thighs. In this position, with her partner's erect penis inside her, the woman rocks backwards and forwards so his penis is stimulating her vagina while her clitoral area rubs against his groin. This ensures maximum genital stimulation for her and a novel and powerful experience for her lover.

▼ **2** From the previous position it is easy for a couple to roll into the side-by-side position to slow the pace and extend their lovemaking – ideal if the man is finding his arousal is ahead of his partner and he's having difficulty keeping control. Now the woman raises her upper leg and wraps it over the man's waist, while keeping her lower leg straight and under her partner's legs. By bending her upper leg she can change the angle of penetration and also pull her partner more tightly towards her. This keeps his movements restricted and prevents him from thrusting too deeply into her.

▼ **3** Still with the woman's upper leg around his waist, the man places his upper leg over his partner's lower thigh so their legs are intertwined. They are now firmly locked together and movement of the pelvis is limited, although they can rock back and forth and gyrate their bodies from the hips to keep the limited amount of stimulation going. In this position they can kiss, and can stroke and caress each other's sides, backs and buttocks. They can also arch their backs away from each other to change the angle of entry and so vary the stimulation they feel. This also pushes their upper bodies apart so the man can stroke and squeeze his partner's breasts and she can stroke his chest.

• **EXPLOSIVE TIP:** *Some women may find their vagina becomes rather dry during extended periods of lovemaking. There are artificial lubricants that can help (see page 65) although simple saliva is a handy alternative.*

▶ **4** The couple can now adjust their position slightly to give themselves more room so that the man can increase the pace and depth of penetration and so bring them both to climax. First the woman raises her upper leg higher so that she is not pulling the man towards her so tightly. This also alters the angle of entry. The man can twist his body slightly so he has more of a downward angle and greater room in order to begin more energetic movements. By resting his upper knee on the bed between his partner's legs he can increase the pace and depth of his thrusts until they both climax.

• **EXPLOSIVE TIP:** *From this position the couple can easily roll over into the man-on-top position if this makes it easier for him to use the rapid, shallow strokes most likely to lead to orgasm.*

EXPLOSIVE FACTS: LOVEMAKING IN LATER LIFE

Provided a couple continue to find each other sexually arousing and still enjoy making love, there is no reason to give up on sexual intimacy just because of advancing years. There are adjustments that need to be made to allow for the physical and physiological changes that come with middle age and beyond, but nothing that can't be solved. For example, to allow for reduced mobility due to back and joint ailments, opt for more relaxed side-by-side positions. Women may discover they now become aroused more quickly whereas men may find it takes longer to power up their libido. Simply by ensuring the man is highly aroused before beginning lovemaking – perhaps by his partner's manual stimulation – a couple can ensure their sexual responses coincide.

SEQUENCE 14

Men and woman vary greatly in how they like to be stimulated during intercourse. This sequence allows the man to vary the angle of penetration so that his partner enjoys a much more varied sexual sensation.

▲ **1** The woman lies on her back and the man separates her legs and kneels between her thighs to enter her. He raises her knees, so that her feet are flat on the bed, and leans forward, placing his hands on the bed for support, to enter her at a lower angle. To change the stimulation he places his hands under her hips to lift her up slightly, and at the same time raises his own body to enter her from a more upright angle (as shown). By switching between the two positions and monitoring her reaction, he should find the angle that offers the most satisfying sensation for her.

▶ **2** If the man takes hold of his partner's calves or ankles and lifts her legs so they are pointing straight up he can raise her bottom off the bed slightly to ensure the head of his penis rubs more effectively against the G-spot on the front wall of her vagina. He can spread her legs apart to widen her vagina (as shown), or place her ankles together and rest them against one shoulder to make the vagina narrower and tighter and so increase the friction. While still with his penis inside his partner and with her ankles together, the man swings her legs to the side so that she is now lying on her side (see inset).

• **EXPLOSIVE TIP:** *If the man now raises his partner's upper leg slightly her bottom and clitoris are accessible to his hand and he can stroke her buttocks or rub her groin as he is thrusting into her to increase the stimulation she receives.*

▲ **3** Now the man lies down behind his partner so they are in the "spoons" position and he can rock back and forth to continue his thrusting movements. He has less freedom of movement than before, which slows the pace of his lovemaking and allows his partner to catch up if she is still not close to climaxing. He can help by reaching round and rubbing her pubic mound and clitoris – through the clitoral hood, if she's very sensitive – as well as her labia and U-spot (see page 55). He can also rub his first and middle finger along her labia in time with his thrusting movements to heighten the sensation. With his other hand he can squeeze and stroke her breasts, a pleasure for both of them.

• **EXPLOSIVE TIP:** *The spoons position, so-called because of the way the two bodies fit together, is powerfully arousing for both partners because of the greater skin-to-skin contact and the fact that the man's hands have easy and generous access to his partner's body.*

▼ **5** In the final stage of this sequence the man rolls his partner onto her front and parts her legs so he can enter her from behind (as shown). By placing a hand under her hips or thighs he can lift her up so that she is partially kneeling and he can thrust into her more easily, increasing the pace and depth of penetration. This brings his penis into contact with another region of her vaginal wall and he may find an area that has never been stimulated before that his partner finds especially arousing.

EXPLOSIVE FACTS: SEX IN PREGNANCY

Being pregnant needn't mean that a couple must abstain from sex until after the birth. Indeed, for a healthy woman with a problem-free pregnancy having sex throughout her term is perfectly natural – and has even been used to bring on an overdue labour. Many women are also more easily aroused at this time. The main exception is for medical reasons, such as a history of previous miscarriage. In that case penetrative sex, especially during the first trimester (three-month period) may be inadvisable. If in doubt, ask your doctor's advice. Even then, oral sex and mutual masturbation may not pose a problem. Towards the end of pregnancy, it is wise to adopt positions that do not put excess pressure on a woman's abdomen, such as woman-on-top, side-by-side and – especially – the "spoons" positions.

SEQUENCE 15

Continuing the theme of "variety adding spice" to lovemaking, this sequence allows a man to vary the angle, depth and rate of his penetration for the ultimate sexual experience.

▼ **1** This sequence begins with the woman lying on her back with her knees raised and the man kneeling between her legs, supporting his upper body on his arms. In this position he can begin slow, shallow thrusting movements that stimulate the outer, more sensitive third of the vagina. By supporting himself on his left arm (for example) he can free up his right hand to stroke and squeeze his partner's breasts – and kiss them too (as shown).

• **EXPLOSIVE TIP:** *In these easy, relaxed opening positions the couple should take every opportunity to gaze into each other's eyes, whisper loving words, and kiss and caress to strengthen the bond between them, an important element for both partners but especially for women.*

▲ **2** Still supporting his body on his right arm, the man reaches behind with his right hand to grip his partner's calf or ankle and lift her left leg up, holding it against his shoulder, while continuing shallow thrusting movements. This changes the angle of his partner's pelvis slightly – allowing him to change direction – and to stimulate a slightly different area of her vagina. In this position his thrusts may cause his groin to rub against his partner's vulva more firmly, increasing the sexual sensations she receives. He can also kiss and caress her leg (as shown).

• **EXPLOSIVE TIP:** *The woman need not remain passive but can stroke her partner's hair, face and neck, showing by these touching romantic gestures how she loves her partner and is enjoying the sensations she is feeling.*

◀ 3 Now the man leans back, supporting his weight on his knees and toes and lifts her left leg up so that both are straight up. By placing his knees on either side of his partner's hips the man can get much closer, allowing for deeper penetration. In this position the man is free to experiment in the different ways he positions his partner's legs. Different positions bring different benefits. By holding her ankles together and pressing her legs against his chest he narrows the vaginal opening, enhancing the rubbing sensation as he thrusts his penis in and out. He can also place her ankles together again and place them first against one shoulder and then the other, moving the angle of her body slightly and varying the area of her vagina that he stimulates.

• **EXPLOSIVE TIP:** *He could also spread his partner's legs very wide, so that more of her vulva is exposed and his groin rubbing against her will increase the stimulation she receives.*

▼ 4 If the man swings both of his partner's legs to one side so that she is lying on her side with her feet resting on the bed he can continue his thrusting movements at a completely different angle. This exposes yet another area of her vagina to the rubbing motion of his penis and may be a sensation his partner has not experienced before. The vaginal opening is tightly closed in this position, which increases the level of friction, and hence stimulation, that both partner's are experiencing. This is a relatively passive position for the woman but she can still turn her head to maintain eye contact and also reach out to stroke her partner's side or thigh.

• **EXPLOSIVE TIP:** *In this position a man can easily stroke his partner's buttocks and legs, and by reaching around her thigh he can rub her clitoris and pubic mound to help bring her to orgasm.*

▲ **5** If the couple want to bring yet more novelty to this sequence, the man can pull his partner's legs out straight behind her and spread them apart so that she is now lying on her front. Her bottom is easily accessible and he can stroke and squeeze her buttocks as he enters her vagina from behind and continues to thrust in and out of her – a highly pleasurable experience for both of them. By laying his body on top of his partner he can increase the skin-to-skin contact they feel and also reach under her to rub and squeeze her breasts and stroke her nipples, or reach down to rub her pubic mound and clitoris.

▶ **6** Now the man places his hands under his partner's hips and lifts her onto his lap, to finish the sequence in the "classic" rear-entry position. The woman can play a more active part in this position by lowering her shoulders, arching her back and lifting her bottom so her partner is stimulating the rear inner wall of her vagina more intensely, or she can sit back in his lap and rock and gyrate her hips in time with his thrusting movements. In this position the man can reach round to stroke and squeeze her breasts or reach down to rub her pubic mound and clitoris to help bring her to orgasm.

• **EXPLOSIVE TIP:** *If the couple are both enjoying the variety of this sequence the man can keep turning his partner and entering her from different angles, finally finishing in the man-on-top position with rapid, shallow thrusts that bring them both to orgasm.*

EXPLOSIVE FACTS: FAKING ORGASMS

It is difficult for a woman to truly fake an orgasm if her partner knows the signs to look for. During an orgasm, her abdominal muscles tighten as rhythmic contractions spread from her vagina and through her pelvic floor. These contractions can be felt by a finger or penis inside her vagina as a steady throb. Her skin will become flushed and she may arch her back and curl her toes. Some women moan, scream, laugh or cry – but many cannot utter a sound even if they wanted to.

SEQUENCE 16

Rear-entry sex, in which the man inserts his penis into his
partner's vagina while he is positioned behind her, can be
powerfully arousing for a man as he is seeing his partner from
a completely different vantage point.

▼ **1** The woman leans over the edge of the bed with her feet on the
floor, supporting her upper body on her arms. The man stands behind
and enter hers, holding his partner's sides, and leans forwards or
backwards to vary the angle and pace of his thrusts.

• **EXPLOSIVE TIP:** *In rear-entry sex the penis mainly rubs against the
less sensitive rear wall of the vagina so varying the angle of penetration
helps enhance the sensation the woman experiences.*

▲ **2** The man places his hands under his partner's thighs to support her while she lifts her legs and wraps them around behind him, pulling him closer with her ankles. The man leans forward and rests his hands on the bed and continues his thrusting movements while his partner gyrates her pelvis to vary the stimulus they experience.

• **EXPLOSIVE TIP:** *In rear-entry sex the penis can easily slip out of the vagina, leading to awkward fumbling as the man re-enters her. By wrapping her legs around him the woman makes it easier for him to stay inside her.*

▲ **3** The woman lowers her arms to flatten herself on the bed, pulling her partner towards her with her ankles. The man leans forward to penetrate her more deeply or stands up straighter and places his hands under her thighs to raise her pelvis off the bed so his penis stimulates the back wall of her vagina more firmly. He can also vary the angle of entry by turning her hips slightly.

• **EXPLOSIVE SEX:** *There is little scope for eye contact during rear entry sex but couples should maintain verbal and tactile communication, talking and reaching out to stroke each other.*

SEQUENCE 17

As a couple discover each other's sexual likes and needs, they begin to develop an intuitive understanding of how to move in their lovemaking that transcends words, and strengthens the bond between them.

▲ 1 This sequence allows a woman to move her body to ensure all parts of her vagina receive the stimulation she craves, while at the same time giving her partner the freedom of action he needs to continue his thrusting movements. It begins in rear-entry position. The man is kneeling and his partner is sitting in his lap with her back towards him. By leaning forwards the woman can give her partner space to thrust his penis into her by rocking on his knees, pushing from his pelvis. The woman gyrates her pelvis to increase the sensation and squeezes her pelvic floor muscles to grip his penis and so enhance the rubbing action.

▲ **2** The woman can then swivel round so she is now sitting sideways in her lover's lap, but with his penis still inside her. Her partner has less freedom of movement in this position. However, if the woman places one arm around his neck and uses the other to support her body on the bed, she can raise her pelvis slightly to help facilitate his thrusts. She can turn towards him to look into his eyes and kiss him, helping to maintain emotional contact. The man can keep one arm around his partner's back to support her while using his other hand to stroke her thighs and squeeze her breasts.

• **EXPLOSIVE TIP:** *In this position the man can easily reach down between his partner's thighs to rub her pubic mound and clitoris to help her to climax.*

▲ **3** Now the woman leans back, supporting herself on her arms while she raises her legs and swivels round to rest them on her partner's shoulders with her ankles locked behind his head. He can help turn her as she makes the transition. The man is now in an easier position to continue his thrusting movements and to increase the pace and depth of his penetration. The woman can help by rocking her hips backwards and forwards to increase the stimulation. She can vary the angle of penetration by pressing her head against the bed and arching her back or pushing herself up, with her arms behind her.

▼ **4** Now the man leans forward and pushes his partner's legs back with his shoulders, lifting her buttocks off the bed as he does so. He can place one arm over her legs to keep her ankles locked around his neck while placing the other hand on the bed to support himself. Now, by raising himself up on his toes he can lift his partner even further off the bed. In this position his penis is rubbing against the front inner wall of his partner's vagina, and especially the G-spot, very strongly. By using his arms to hold his partner's legs together he is closing her vagina tightly around his penis, increasing the friction for maximum stimulation. The woman can dictate how close the man presses down on her by placing an arm around his neck to pull him closer or pressing her hands against his chest to push him back.

EXPLOSIVE FACTS: THE BRIDGE TECHNIQUE

Some women find they cannot climax through penetrative sex alone, no matter which position they try. Of course, all orgasms are good – whether achieved through penetration or through a combination of manual and oral stimulation. However, for women who feel they are missing out by not climaxing through penetrative intercourse, sex therapists and relationship counsellors often recommend they try the "bridge" technique. Here the man uses any form of stimulation his partner finds arousing, including manual stimulation, oral sex, and even sex toys, such as a vibrator, until the woman is close to having an orgasm. He then inserts his penis and brings her to climax through a combination of penile thrusting and manual stimulation, for example by rubbing her clitoris. This is easier if they adopt a position such as rear-entry so that the woman's vulva is more easily accessible.

SEQUENCE 18

For wild, lust-filled, spontaneous do-it-anywhere sex, when both partners are so highly aroused they can barely wait to tear each other's clothes off, the ultimate thrill is to make love standing up.

▼ **1** This is a great position for adventurous couples to adopt in any room in the house, other than the bedroom. As the man and woman stand kissing their hands are free to caress each other's ears, neck and chest. The man can squeeze his partner's breasts and rub her pubic mound and vulva with his palm, before pushing a finger into her vagina to stimulate her further.

EXPLOSIVE FACTS: MULTIPLE ORGASMS

A woman may need as much as 15 minutes stimulation before climaxing – up to five times as long as a man. As compensation, her orgasm may last up to five times as long as his – more than a minute in some cases. If a woman is stimulated around 20 seconds after having an orgasm she may become re-aroused and climax again (and again) more quickly than before. This is known as multiple orgasm. As a woman begins to discover more about her body and its sexual responses – and with the help of an understanding partner – multiple orgasms become the norm and not the exception.

▼ **2** When the woman wants to take their intimacy to the next stage she raises one leg to waist level. If she locks her ankle behind her partner she can pull them tightly together. The man places his hand under her thigh for support. In this position the woman's legs are spread wide, which opens her vulva even more for his hand to continue to explore her body. With deft touches of his fingers he can bring his partner to a heightened state of arousal before finally entering her. Placing his hands around her waist to keep her close he can rock his pelvis to begin rhythmic thrusting movements.

▼ **3** He now places both hands under his partner's buttocks or behind her back (as shown) to support her, allowing her to raise her other leg and place both thighs on either side of his waist, while he uses a rocking motion to thrust in and out of her. By pressing her abdomen against her partner the woman can move her pelvis backwards and forwards to match his movements. They can continue in this position for as long as he can support her, or lay her down on a sofa or bed and continue penetrative sex until they climax.

SEQUENCE 19

Once you develop a taste for standing sex there are many
variations you can try to heighten the experience. This
sequence is based on a famous Kama Sutra position and
requires a convenient wall…

▲ **1** The couple stand facing each other, kissing and petting, with the
man's back towards a wall. He places his hands under his partner's thighs,
and she puts her hands behind his neck and raises one thigh so he can
enter her. When ready, the woman raises both legs off the ground,
supported by her partner. It may be easier for the woman if she places
her hands behind her partner's neck.

▲ **2** She now straightens her legs to place her feet against the wall. With the wall for leverage, she can rock her pelvis in time with her partner's pelvic thrusts. She can also grind her pelvic mound and clitoris into his groin and squeeze her pelvic floor muscles around his penis to enhance the sensation. If the woman still has confidence in her partner's strength she can lean back even farther.

• **EXPLOSIVE TIP:** *This is a physically demanding sequence for a man and he will need plenty of verbal encouragement from his partner if he is to keep going until they climax.*

▲ **3** By placing her feet higher on the wall, while leaning back further, the woman can "walk" up the wall, changing the angle of penetration and the area of her vagina being stimulated. The couple can stay like this for as long as the man's strength can hold out – until they climax, if they wish. Alternatively the woman can pull herself back into a straighter position and put her hands around his neck again.

• **EXPLOSIVE TIP:** *The man can use this sequence purely as an exciting preliminary before laying his partner on a flat surface such as a table for impromptu sex in the kitchen or dining room.*

SEQUENCE 20

This sequence is for highly athletic couples who enjoy including the spirit of adventure in their lovemaking and want to try positions that are both physically and sexually demanding. Don't try this unless you are very fit and supple…

▼ **1** You should choose a soft surface such as a carpeted floor (or lawn – if daring enough to try this in the garden!). Supported by her partner's hands under her buttocks, the woman hops up into his arms and wraps her legs around his waist.

• **EXPLOSIVE TIP:** *For safety, clear the floor of obstructions and keep away from furniture or other objects. Scatter pillows or cushions behind the woman so she has a soft landing in case of mishap!*

EXPLOSIVE FACTS:
DELAYED EJACULATION

Being able to delay ejaculation is an important skill but some men actually find it difficult to climax – even after extended periods of lovemaking, perhaps through being over-stimulated. If so it can help to pause briefly – just long enough to allow the erection to subside – before becoming re-aroused. This delay may relax the man just enough to "tip him over the edge" so he can climax.

▲ **2** The woman places her hands behind her partner's neck as he pushes his penis into her. By crossing her ankles behind her partner the woman can lock her legs so she can pull herself closer to him and is securely supported before attempting the next move. Releasing her hands from his neck she leans right back and places her hands on the floor. The man may need to lean back in the opposite direction to act as counter balance and bend his legs so his partner doesn't have to stretch too far. Thrusting movements are limited in this position but the man can provide some stimulation by rocking his pelvis backwards and forwards.

▲ **3** The woman can take this move even further by arching her back and resting the top of her head on the floor, supported by her hands pressed flat – or just her head (as shown). The man can bend his knees to help her and provide extra support for her lower back. The woman can grip his calves for support. This exciting and unique position provides an arousing preliminary before switching to an easier position for sex.

• **EXPLOSIVE TIP:** *In this extreme position the rush of blood to the head that women experience can take their sexual arousal to far greater heights and lead to explosive orgasms!*

SEQUENCE 21

Many couples turn to Tantric sex to take their lovemaking to a higher level. The time couples spend together in this position enhances the relationship by strengthening the spiritual union between them.

▼ **1** From the first step in Tantric sex, the aim is to develop a sense of spiritual and emotional union. The man and woman take up a kneeling position facing each other and look into each other's eyes. They place their left hands together, palm-to-palm and right hands over each other's heart. Now they slow their breathing, drawing each breath from deep in their lungs and focus on their partner's heartbeat and breathing, as felt through their hands.

EXPLOSIVE FACTS: DIVINE SEX

Many couples who enjoy a full, active and varied sex life feel there's something missing. Having reached the pinnacle of sexual fulfilment they want to take their relationship to another, spiritual dimension. This is the essence of "Tantra" or Tantric sex, based on a fusion of Hindu and Buddhist texts. Tantric sex recreates the divine couplings of the Hindu deities to achieve physical and spiritual union. In order to achieve the ultimate state of bliss, it is important to prepare the mind as well as the body. This is achieved through meditation and by focusing on your partner's heartbeat and breathing.

▼ **2** After spending time allowing their breathing to synchronize, the woman lifts herself onto her partner's lap. The couple hold this pose while continuing to synchronize breathing. The couple look into each other's eyes and imagine they are breathing their partner in, developing the same steady rhythm. After a while they may find that, along with their breathing, their pulse rates synchronize too. The couple now close their eyes but continue to focus their thoughts on each other. They are becoming sexual and emotional soul mates – two hearts beating as one.

▼ **3** Now the woman wraps her legs around her partner as he enters her and they hold each other closer. With practise they can maintain this position for increasingly long periods using minimal rocking motions of their pelvis. The man can move his penis just enough to bring both of them to a slow, steady state of sexual arousal. In this position the man's groin rubs against his partner's clitoris, providing additional stimulus. She can use her pelvic floor muscles to squeeze his penis and maintain his erection. The couple can stay like this to orgasm or, when ready, switch to another position.

SEQUENCE 22

There are many positions for Tantric sex, some borrowed from
the Kama Sutra (see page 88). They are all very demanding
and require couples to be supple. However they also provide
a unique form of sexual stimulus.

▲ **I** The man and woman sit on the bed or floor facing each other. The
man sits with his knees apart and feet together. The woman sits between
her partner's thighs with her legs around his waist. Now she pulls herself
closer to her partner so he can penetrate her. By crossing her ankles
behind the man she can pull them both tightly together. Both partners
then rock their hips back and forth, in synchrony.

▶ **2** The woman now lies back, supporting herself on her hands, and arches her back. In this position the man's penis is rubbing against the front inner wall of her vagina, giving more stimulation, while the restricted position limits his movement to slow shallow thrusts. The woman can contract her pelvic floor muscles around his penis to increase the stimulation while slowing the pace even more. The couple maintain eye contact, helping to strengthen a sense of emotional and spiritual "oneness", matching their breathing with the slow pace of their movements.

▶ **3** Now the man leans back too, supporting himself on one hand and his partner's lower back with the other. Using one hand and his feet for leverage he pushes up from his hips and arches his back to raise his pelvis and lift his partner off the bed. They now close their eyes and meditate, focusing on the sexual sensations they feel. By rocking back and forth in unison they continue the stimulation, keeping their breaths deep and slow and synchronizing their pelvic movements with their breathing. For novice couples, this is a demanding position and they may not be able to sustain it for long before switching to another pose.

SEQUENCE 23

This sequence completes the Tantric section by allowing a couple to release their sexual energy in an explosive simultaneous orgasm. It includes the classic Kama Sutra position "Wife of Indrani" (consort of a Hindu god).

▼ **1** The man takes up a kneeling position and his partner sits on his lap, leaning back with her legs around his waist, as in step 1 of the previous sequence (see page 94), and they follow the steps to synchronize heart rate and breathing. As they feel a sense of spiritual "oneness" the woman locks her ankles behind the man's back to pull herself closer to him so that he can penetrate her. They wrap their arms around each other, placing their heads together and begin to rock, synchronizing their movements at a slow steady pace. The woman uses her pelvic floor muscles to help maintain her partner's erection.

EXPLOSIVE FACTS: RIDING THE WAVE

The ultimate aim of Tantric sex is to delay orgasm in order to harness the sexual energy that is being generated by orgasm. This leads to an emotional and physical high known as "riding the wave". After much practise, Tantric devotees maintain this state for hours. For novice couples, though, it is sufficient to increase the time normally taken to climax – if only by minutes. By extending their lovemaking at each session they may be able to "ride the wave" for an hour or more.

▲ **2** Now the woman places her arms behind her and lowers her head and shoulders until they are touching the bed. Her partner can support her by placing a hand behind her back and leaning forward to help lower her gently while still keeping his penis inside her. The woman uncrosses her ankles and places her feet flat on the bed. Now the man grips his partner's ankles and raises her legs, bending her knees and placing her feet against his forehead.

▼ **3** The man crosses his partner's legs in front of her and leans forward to press her legs gently against her chest, a position known as "Wife of Indrani". The woman can control how far back he presses her by pushing against his shoulder. This position gives the man more freedom of movement, varying from slow deep thrusts to more rapid shallow ones. He can also change the angle of penetration so his partner is receiving more varied stimulation. If the couple are completely in tune with one another they may achieve a powerful simultaneous orgasm.

FUN & GAMES 3

"Really, sex and laughter do go very well
together, and I wondered
(and still do) which is more important."
Hermione Gingold

If there's a naughty notion or wicked whim that you've been
dying to try but didn't feel you even dare raise the subject
then now is the time. Your partner will probably be as eager
as you to try them too and may have super-sexy suggestions
of their own to offer.

Your fun is limited only by the power of your imagination. If
nothing else, it will give you both a good laugh and put you in
the mood for uninhibited lovemaking. Whether through sexy
games of chance or dressing up, erotic fantasy and roll play or
sexual sensation games, there are lots of fun ways to keep the
joie de vivre in your relationship.

The following pages feature toe-tingling ideas to start you off.
But you'll soon come up with super sinful suggestions of your
own that are just as wickedly wanton – if not more so! You'll
soon be giggling like children as you indulge in these very
adult activities…

ROLE-PLAYING

On the following pages you'll find fun encounters of the adult kind… Sex games add sparkle to a relationship by providing new laughs, new thrills, new sensations and new ways of behaving.

Why not start with a little role-play? Pretend you're meeting for the first time. Set up a small table with intimate lighting to mimic a cosy corner in your favourite bar or café. One partner is sitting having a drink when the other casually wanders over and asks to share the table. As you chat, your conversation becomes more and more intimate.

Perhaps your partner is wearing a coat, which she casually allows to fall open revealing sexy underwear – or nothing at all. Sitting closer together you begin to explore each other's body surreptitiously, under the table. See how long you can keep the seduction going until your passion forces you to take it further.

You could try role-play of a different kind. The woman could be a lap dancer, in her sexiest most sparkly outfit and her partner one of her eager clients. Her job is to drive him wild with her sexy moves while he can only watch and yearn but mustn't touch.

Below Left Indulge the secret performer in you by imagining you are a lap dancer. Entertain your partner with some sultry dance steps, while he sits back and enjoys the show.

Below Right Become the ultimate club-night temptress and drive him wild with desire as you grind your body into his.

DRESSING UP FOR SEX

Clothes not only change the way we look but also affect the way we feel and behave. By dressing up you hide your normal persona and let different aspects of your personality emerge from the shadows. You can be whoever you want to be and, as this is not the real you, indulge your naughtiest sexual fantasies without fear of embarrassment.

The simplest disguise is the mask – as worn at a masked ball or masquerade. You're now a figure of mystery, free to do what you like without guilt or fear of the consequences. This is a new you who is not tied by old rules of behaviour, so indulge yourself. It is a treat for your partner, too, who now has a mystery lover to indulge his or her fantasies.

You can hire fancy dress costumes or create your own fantasy personality using the clothes you already have. You just need a little imagination. For example, dress up as a high-class escort girl or gigolo

Above If you dream of a fantasy figure ask your partner to put on a masquerade mask, then they can be anyone you want them to be and no one even needs to know who that is.

Above By putting on a fantasy nurse's outfit you can expose the nurturing side of your nature – clearly your patient is in need of some TLC of the sexual kind, and only you can provide it.

Right Dressing up as a French maid might help you to unlock the naughty side of your nature – one who is happy to combine work and play.

and cast all moral codes to the wind. A woman only needs a short or split skirt, stockings and low-cut top. A man can wear an expensive tuxedo with silk shirt open to the waist (medallion optional). As a lady or gentleman "of the night", your task is simple: perform whatever sexual services your "client" demands.

Some clothes are naturally sexy. Nice girls love a sailor, but naughty ones also go for a fireman, dispatch rider, builder, whatever… A nurse's starched uniform or French maid's outfit of frilly knickers, short skirt and stockings may seem corny but can still work their sexual magic for wearer and viewer. School uniform suggests vulnerability and wide-eyed innocence. Any situation where you must do as you're told, means you are free of blame and can give your conscience the night off, submitting to whatever you're expected to do.

Adopt the uniform of an authority figure such as a police officer or customs official and wield power with impunity. The rule of this game is that the dominant party sets the rules and the submissive one obeys without question – from fear of punishment. Take turns so that both of you experience the pleasure of total immoral power.

> *"Don't worry. It only seems kinky the first time."*
> Sigmund Freud

You can star in your own erotic movie by creating a sex scenario – such as doctors and nurses, the randy repairman, a sexy secretary with her sex-starved boss, cops and robbers, or whatever you like. If you use a camcorder you can show your movie on your TV, creating a magic moment you can view again and again. For a less permanent effect, place a few free-standing mirrors in strategic positions around the bed so you can watch yourselves making love from new, exciting and previously unseen angles.

What about cross-dressing for role reversal with a difference? If a man likes the feel of his partner's body through a delicate garment he may be curious to know how that soft silky material feels against his own skin. A man can then explore the feminine side of his nature during lovemaking, with his partner taking a more dominant role.

Being able to set the rules is a powerful turn-on for women. But why stop there? If the desire to dominate has taken hold, wear leather and ultra-high heels to become a dominatrix and give your lover the punishment he richly deserves…

Left For the ultimate sexual tease, imagine your partner as a law officer who is searching for contraband – who knows where he will find it?

Right Fantasy fun is limited only by the power of your imagination. A simple leather jacket can transform your partner into the Easy Rider of your dreams, ready to whisk you away.

HANKY SPANKY

Chastisement is the name of this game. There are good erotic reasons to inflict mild pain, such as gentle bites, scratches, slaps or smacks, on your partner. Mild pain energizes the sexual nerve endings and enhances the erotic stimulation that follows. Those are all perfectly valid reasons to spank your partner but there's a better one – it's good fun!

Remember, though, sexual chastisement is a sign of affection and an arousing addition to your erotic repertoire. It is not an excuse to settle old scores. If you plan to hit your partner quite hard then reserve your smacks for buttocks and the backs of thighs. These fleshy areas can absorb slaps without injury and, best of all, are key erotic regions.

Use the flat of the fingers (not the palms) to deliver a few slaps – counting at least six between each one (vary the timing to increase the suspense). Make your actions energizing – not agonizing – just hard enough to make the skin glow, then rub and kiss the area better.

Try scratching and biting your partner, but – to avoid later embarrassment – keep to areas that do not usually show. Run

Below Satisfy your desire to be dominant, and your partner's secret wish to be submissive, by putting on some thigh-length boots and making your man do as he's told.

your nails along your partner's back or buttocks, hard enough to make slight indentations and leave little white lines but not enough to break the skin. Make little patterns, love hearts or figures-of-eight, and kiss them. Apply your teeth to fleshy areas such as thighs, buttocks, shoulders and upper arms. Bite hard enough to leave a mark but, again, take care not to damage the skin.

A LITTLE TIED UP…

For sexual teasing try bondage games. Tie your partner's hands behind their back or anchor them to the bedstead until your lover is helplessly at your mercy. Then tie a scarf or blindfold over their eyes so they can't guess what you're about to do until you do it.

Chastise your partner with impunity, if you wish, before running your hands over their body. As your partner is helpless you can tease your partner to make the sexual torture even more exquisite. Take your time,; after all, he or she is not going anywhere.

Start by tickling. Everyone has a ticklish spot, even men, and if you don't know where it is you'll have fun finding it. Use a feather to increase the pleasure – this can be a huge turn-on for women, though be prepared for loud squeals and giggles. Use slow, light strokes, drawing the feather over thighs, buttocks or abdomen and around chest or breasts and nipples before sliding down to stroke the belly, thighs and vulva, or penis and testicles.

Above Take turns to administer the punishment. With her hands tied behind her back she is powerless to prevent your chastisement but always remember to kiss it better afterwards.

Below With your partner bound and blindfolded you are free to do what you like, including oral arousal. It can be the ultimate in sexual torture… of the nicest kind of course.

Above Experiment with various sensations on different parts of the body. Lightly pressing an ice cube on to sensitive areas is an arousing experience, especially when it is followed by melted candle wax.

SENSUAL SENSATIONS

Experiment with other sexy sensations by using a soft hairbrush, melted wax, ice cubes, a feather, or anything else handy. The skin is packed with nerve endings, all responding to slightly different stimuli. You won't be able to discover all the sensual delights that you can enjoy unless you experiment.

Stock up on energy foods to give your lovemaking a boost. Items such as chocolate, oysters and champagne are traditional aphrodisiacs that boost a lover's ardour when consumed before lovemaking. But for a real feast, use your partner as a dinner plate! Turn your partner into a sushi bar or smorgasbord by placing favourite treats on their back or belly and – using your lips alone – pick them off and eat them. Take your time for an arousing repast. Try sexily sticky treats such as whipped cream, melted chocolate, or honey – anything that feels deliciously sensual when applied to breasts or abdomen. Ice cream is a chilly delight when smoothed over nipples and slowly removed by tongue.

Perhaps you've longed for a relaxing sensual – and sexual – massage, but never knew where to start. Demonstrate on your partner first so he can learn the technique (see *Sexual Massage* on page 110) and can then apply it to you. If he knows that no part of your body is off limits he won't need much persuading. To make it a game, though, the masseur (or masseuse) must see how long they can keep from fondling the main pleasure zones, and how long they can keep their partner aroused before they climax.

Left Try stroking a feather lightly over your partner's body to find sexually sensitive regions that they may not even know they had. The more erogenous the zone, the more erotic the sensation.

Below Chocolate dripped on the skin is a gooey delight in itself, but the best is yet to come when your body becomes the ultimate fantasy feast, as your partner takes his time licking it off.

SEXUAL MASSAGE

Sexual massage is not only great fun it is a good way to ease tension and get you and your partner in the mood for love and laughter, especially after a stressful day. The only difference between sexual massage and the conventional "sensual" kind is that all parts of the body are included.

Remember, though, this is massage, not sex (that comes later!) so give all parts of the body your full attention and avoid the main erogenous zones at first or the massage will be over all too soon. Baby oil, olive oil or almond oil help the hands glide over the skin and bring your partner's senses alive — spread towels on the bed to avoid leaving oily stains — or opt for talcum powder instead.

The best kind of sexual massage is relaxed and spontaneous, though, so all you need is an eager masseur and a compliant body. Use smooth gliding movements with the pads of your fingers. Adapt your strokes to different parts of the body: sweeping moves for larger areas of flesh and soft, feather-like strokes on smaller, more delicate regions.

Below It is fun to run your hands over your partner's body, but there is also a more serious side to massage. A skilful masseur can help ease away their lover's stress and prepare them for a night of relaxed romance.

Right Keep the massage going until you have found all the areas of tension and smoothed them away, then your partner will be ready for the erotic pleasures to come.

1 With your partner lying on their tummy, use broad strokes that fan out from the lower back up to the shoulders. Continue over arms, shoulders and thighs, working towards the heart.

2 Follow up with a firm squeezing or kneading action on fleshy areas of the thighs, upper arms and – especially – buttocks.

3 Use firm circular strokes on areas of muscle tension and delicate, circular strokes on neck and feet.

4 Now turn your partner over so they are lying on their back. Repeat the sweeping movements that you used before but, again, avoid the main erogenous zones – for now. Keep the movements slow and rhythmic. Try a firmer squeezing action on the chest or breasts and gently stroke the nipples with your fingertips.

5 Vary your pressure and pace, and be guided by your partner's responses. If you feel your partner tense up, make your touch a little gentler.

6 When the moment is right, focus on your partner's genitals. A woman can slowly part her lover's legs and stroke the inside of his thighs up to his perineum, before cupping and gently squeezing his testicles. Then she can stroke his penis, making him come erect – if he isn't already. When ready she can masturbate him or switch to oral stimulation (see page 26).

7 The man can part his partner's legs and stroke her perineum before exploring her vulva. He can stimulate her manually or arouse her with his mouth and tongue (see page 28). Or sexual massage can simply be a prelude to other types of fun and games – it's your call…

BAWDY BOARD GAMES

If you want to add a chance element to your fun then make a real game of it. The most famous sex game is strip poker. Here you bet with items of clothing, such as a scarf or tie for openers, slowly working down to your underwear. If you don't know the rules of poker then adapt a game that you do know such as strip snap – where the loser takes off an item of their opponent's choosing.

The aim of a strip game is to see your opponent naked, of course, which is a good enough reason to play it in itself. But why stop there? Instead of clothes you could bet sexual services, such as fondling your partner's breasts or testicles (or being fondled), masturbating your partner (or being masturbated), or oral sex. You get the idea.

You could write down all the sexy ideas you can think of on pieces of paper and give them a value – just like money. The larger the wager the more intimate the task the loser must perform. For "big money" deals there are the fantastic positions and permutations featured in *Chapter 2* of this book.

Below Strip poker is a great way to get your partner naked, but why stop there? Take the game a step further by betting "dares" that the loser must perform. The larger the bet, the more risqué the dare.

Far Right Once luck takes a hand in your romantic moments there is no knowing where it will lead. Think up some outrageous activities that you will both enjoy… and see what fate decides.

DICE GAMES

Instead of cards, try throwing dice. Each number that two dice can produce could represent a different part of the body to be squeezed, stroked, licked or sucked. There are 11 possible permutations, from two ones (2) to two sixes (12). Take turns to throw the dice and, whatever number appears, that is the part that receives your lover's attention.

Alternatively you could choose 11 different popular sexual activities. Number them 2 to 12 and, take turns to throw the dice. Whatever number turns up (say, 3 + 4 = 7) that is the one you perform (see page 114). For a double six you could throw the dice again to include yet more sexy options in your list.

If you're feeling particularly brave, you could dare each other to attempt more adventurous activities or positions that you and your partner have been too shy or inhibited to try, such as standing sex or sex in the open air. If the throw of the dice so decides then you know it is all down to the fickle finger of fate and you have no choice but to obey – the perfect excuse to release your inner sex demon.

"Remember, if you smoke after sex you're doing it too fast."
Woody Allen

"There is nothing wrong with making love with the light on. Just make sure the car door is closed."
George Burns

AL FRESCO FUN

The word "al fresco" literally means "in the fresh" but has come to mean "open air". Al fresco lovemaking is the ultimate turn on. It carries the risk, of course, of being spied on by others or arrested. For some people that is all part of the thrill. It is not for the timid, easily embarrassed or those whose jobs require a strict code of behaviour and for whom any scandal would mean career suicide.

That said, with a little care and discretion all couples can enjoy the freedom and pleasure of love in the sun or under the stars with little risk. You could begin close to home by spreading out a blanket on your garden lawn. Choose a place that is shielded by shrubs or put up screens or a gazebo to hide you from prying eyes. Then all you have to worry about is a passing police helicopter or balloonist. If you reserve your tryst for the hours of darkness then even this risk is avoided.

For more adventurous assignations park your car in a secluded country lane and kiss and cuddle like illicit lovers. Then grab a blanket and head into the trees to consummate your passion. Woodland is ideal for al fresco sex. A cushion of leaves beneath you, dappled light shimmering through the branches and the breeze in the trees provide a feast for the senses that will enhance your lovemaking. The foliage also affords cover from prying eyes and you'll be able to hear approaching footsteps from a long way off.

SEX TOYS AND PLAY CHESTS

Sex shops now have a wide range of toys for use in sex games and to enhance sexual pleasure. Instead of going clothes shopping, take your partner "sex shopping" instead. Even if you don't buy anything, an hour or so perusing the shelves should provide some sizzling suggestions to try when you get home. Sex shops also offer devices such as whips, canes or paddles designed specifically for mild (or "vanilla") pseudo-sado-masochistic games, if you want to take chastisement to another level.

If you stock up on sex toys, keep them in a special "sex chest". Use a storage box, or reserve a drawer in a dressing table or wardrobe for all your sexual aids (see *Stocking Your Sex Chest*, right). If you use condoms, keep them here along with a box of tissues. That way you'll be able to find everything you need in a hurry when your libido is rising.

Below What you get up to in the privacy of your own home is completely up to you, so be creative. Masks, whips, paddles and handcuffs are all fun accessories that are easy to find and buy, and can help keep things exciting.

EXPLOSIVE FUN: STOCKING YOUR SEX CHEST

Popular sex toys include dice with sexy words or pictures of sex positions instead of dots, fur-lined handcuffs for chafe-free bondage games, silk scarves to blindfold or bind your lover, and canes, whips and paddles for chastisement. Include in your intimate play chest a CD of sexy music and scented candles to enhance the romantic mood. You could also include erotic magazines or DVDs. All sex shops have a bewildering array of devices to enhance your sexual pleasure, too many to list here. The most popular are the dildo and vibrator. As its name suggests, a vibrator is a battery-powered instrument that vibrates, and some wriggle as well. Vibrators come in all shapes, sizes and textures. As well as traditional dildo- or penis-like ones, there are ball- or egg-shaped devices and multiheaded types that can stimulate several erogenous zones at once.

GOOD VIBRATIONS

For women who find it difficult to climax through penetration, or manual or oral stimulation, alone then a vibrator may be the answer. Men, too, will find a vibrator enhances their sexual pleasure. Before applying the vibrator to your partner's genital regions, use it to explore all of your lover's erogenous zones.

Areas of your skin that have never come alive before can generate electrifying sensations when a vibrator is applied. Try running it along your partner's thighs, working up and down the outer part of the leg before doing the same thing to the inner thigh. Now apply it to abdomen, buttocks, chest/breasts and – of course – the nipples.

Those areas of heightened sensitivity on a woman that usually produce a powerful sexual response may be too sensitive to be stimulated with a vibrator directly. These include the inner and outer labia, the U-spot (see page 55) and, of course, the clitoris. You'll only discover this by applying the vibrator and seeing her response.

Women often find it easier to have vaginal orgasms using a vibrator, especially when placed against the G-spot (see page 46) or deeper down towards the A-spot (see page 49). Vibrators vary in width and length so unless you know for sure what size is best for you, start with a narrow one and work up to the optimum size.

> *"Sex is the most fun I ever had*
> *without laughing."*
> Woody Allen

For men, vibrators rarely provide enough stimulation to bring about an orgasm on their own but may help them become re-aroused when they've already ejaculated. A vibrator also enhances a man's pleasure when combined with manual or oral stimulation. His partner can rub it over different areas of his body, such as the perineum and testicles, the shaft of the penis – paying particular attention to the frenulum – and over the glans.

Any children's game can be adapted to an adult theme, including the old party favourite of "sardines" (a variation of "hide and seek"). Flip a coin to decide who hides, then the quarry must choose somewhere confined such as a closet or under the bed. The seeker counts to 50 before looking for them. If successful, the seeker joins the quarry in the hiding place. It is the seeker who chooses what they do there and the quarry who decides how much space they will have to do it in. Now you have the idea, think of some sexy suggestions of your own to try…

Right There is nothing quite so versatile as a vibrator. You can apply it to all parts of your partner's body to produce the most highly charged sexual sensations. You don't have to tie your partner up first, unless you want to…

CARTE DU JOUR:

A GLOSSARY OF SEXUAL TERMS AND TREATS

"It is not sex that gives the
pleasure, but the lover."
Marge Piercy

A-SPOT

A highly sexually responsive area that is located well inside the vagina close to the cervix (neck of the uterus) and hence is only stimulated during deep penetrative sex. Also called the anterior fornix erogenous zone, it was first described by Malaysian scientist Dr Chua Chee Ann.

ANAL SEX

Penetrative sex where the penis is inserted into the anus rather than the vagina. It can be less arousing for a woman, who will need additional clitoral stimulation to achieve an orgasm, but it does offer a unique sexual experience for both partners.

APHRODISIAC

Any food, drink or drug that stimulates arousal. Popular aphrodisiacs include oysters, artichokes and chocolate. Romantic treats in Mediterranean countries include baked almonds, while in East Asia, food containing ginger, cinnamon and ginseng are regarded as aphrodisiac. Alcohol is a common aphrodisiac as it suppresses inhibitions.

AUSTRALIAN

Any sexual position in which a woman's head is below the level of her body. The rush of blood to her head can enhance her sexual high. One position is if she lies with her head and shoulders over the end of the bed.

BURGUNDIAN

A sexual position in which a woman lies on her back and raises her legs high enough to wrap her ankles around her partner's neck, it allows deep penetration.

CLAMPS

Small clips that are most often placed on the nipples and genitals, clamps can be adjusted to various tensions to induce mild or more painful sensations.

CLITORIS

The highly sexually responsive, button-like structure in the vulva that is located where the two inner labia meet. Usually covered by a hood of skin, it lengthens and stiffens during arousal. Clitoral stimulation with a finger, palm of the hand, lips or tongue is an effective way for women to climax.

COITAL ALIGNMENT TECHNIQUE

The "CAT" is a combined sexual position and rocking motion that ensures the man's pubic bone rubs against his partner's clitoris to enhance the sexual stimulation she receives during penetrative sex.

COWGIRL

Sexual position in which the woman straddles her partner as though she is riding a horse, in order to control their lovemaking. By rocking her pelvis she can maximize the level of stimulation she receives. For the "reverse cowgirl" position she sits facing the opposite direction, looking towards her partner's feet.

CUISSADE

Sexual position that combines rear-entry with side entry to take advantage of the benefits of both positions. The woman lies with one leg between her partner's legs and the other drawn up across her abdomen. It enhances stimulation for her, while also slowing the man's movements.

CUNNILINGUS

Oral sex performed on a woman, in which the mouth stimulates the vulva.

EROGENOUS ZONE

Any erotically sensitive body part that excites sexual arousal when stimulated. Common erogenous zones, aside from the genitals, are breasts/chest, buttocks, thighs and perineum.

EROTICA

Any literature or photography or film that depicts sex, erotica can be an exciting precursor to lovemaking.

FEATHERS

Used for stimulating the breasts, buttocks, genitals, thighs and even the palms of the hands and soles of the feet. Soft peacock feathers lend an exotic air, but stiff wiry feathers or "mops" are more effective.

FELLATIO

Oral sex performed on a man, in which the mouth stimulates the penis.

FETISH

Sexual desire where gratification is fixated on a specific clothing item, object, activity or body part. Common fetishes include wearing rubber, leather, high-heeled shoes, lacy underwear, and being spanked. Feet are common fetish body parts. Incorporating your personal turn-ons and your partner's fetishes into your lovemaking is an easy and effective way to keep sex exciting and interesting.

FIGHT-PLAY

Pretend fighting can be a turn on and bring energy into your lovemaking. Many couples enjoy extended physical struggles for foreplay, such as love wrestling, pillow fights, and playful slaps and spanks. Actual violence should not be tolerated.

FIRE AND ICE

Alternating hot and cold sensations on the skin to activate different sets of nerve endings and so sensitise the skin as an aid to sexual arousal. For example, ice cubes rubbed on the skin is alternated with melted wax dripped from a plain unscented candle on to any hairless area of the body. Always test the heat of the wax on your arm first.

FISTING

Pushing a fist into the vagina or anus. Full-hand penetration takes much practice and trust by both partners. Apply plenty of lubrication before you start, and never use force.

FLAGELLATION

Act of whipping or flogging a person for sexual arousal, usually as part of sadomasochistic or dominant/submissive sexual activities.

FLANQUETTE

Half-facing sexual posture in which each partner has one leg between the other partner's two legs and one leg outside (interleaved). It provides clitoral stimulation but inhibits deep penetration and so is mainly used to slow the pace during lovemaking.

FOREPLAY

Sexual stimulation of erogenous zones, using the hands and/or the mouth, up to (or including) orgasm. Usually a preliminary to other forms of sex, it is a particularly important element of lovemaking for women, who may need 15 minutes or more stimulation to be aroused.

FRENULUM

Highly sexually responsive area on the underside of the penis, where shaft and head (glans) meet. It is powerfully arousing for a man when stimulated by a woman during mutual masturbation or oral sex.

FRONTAL

Any face-to-face position where one partner places both legs between the other partner's legs. Such positions may enable deep penetration but offer limited clitoral stimulation.

FROTTAGE

Sexual stimulation through genital rubbing but without penetration. Can be performed clothed or unclothed and involve any body part, including the abdomen, buttocks, breasts, thighs, feet or genitals. It is used as foreplay or to achieve orgasm without oral, vaginal or anal sexual intercourse.

G-SPOT

Highly sexually responsive region on the front wall of the vagina, about 5 cm (2 in) from the vaginal entrance. In some women G-spot stimulation is the key to achieving an orgasm, for others it simply intensifies the sensation, or it may have little effect.

GAG

Cloth, strap or other device used in sex games to engender feelings of helplessness and submission. Take care when using a gag – ensure it doesn't hinder breathing and can be removed quickly if a partner is in distress.

GLANS

Head of penis and its most sensitive part. The glans is covered by a foreskin unless the man is circumcised.

GLUTEAL SEX

Sexual practice in which the penis is moved between the crease of the partner's buttocks without being inserted in the anus. The woman contracts her gluteal muscles and rocks her pelvis to increase friction.

GOURMET SEX

Wild, uninhibited sex in which both partners ensure the other is sexually satisfied. It may boost sperm levels significantly and so is ideal for couples who are trying to conceive.

JESUS CROSS

Sexual position in which a woman lies flat on top of her partner and with her back to him, while he penetrates her vagina from behind.

LABIA

Latin name for the two sets of lip-like structures that surround the vagina. The fleshy outer lips are known as the labia majora and the more delicate inner lips are called the labia minora.

LAP DANCE

A seductive dance performed for a seated client.

MASSAGE

A full-body massage can be an unhurried, relaxing way to get in the mood for lovemaking or used as foreplay and incorporate the massage of the breasts and genitals. It can include the use of vibrators and battery-operated massage tools.

MASTURBATION

Manual sexual stimulation of the genitals, usually to orgasm. When partners perform this on each other it is called mutual masturbation.

MATRIMONIAL

A form of missionary position where the woman wraps her legs around he partner's waist to pull him closer. It allows her to control her partner's thrusting movements and direct his penis towards the most sensitive areas of her vagina.

MIRROR MOVIE

A carefully placed, full-length mirror that allows couples to watch themselves while they are making love, as though they are viewing themselves taking part in a porn movie.

MISSIONARY

Face-to-face sex position in which the man lies between his partner's legs, usually supporting himself on his hands or forearms. It offers lots of skin-to-skin contact and, by changing the position of his body, he can vary the angle of his thrusts to satisfy his partner.

MONS PUBIS

Fleshy mound at the base of a woman's abdomen, just above the vulva. It is a major erogenous zone, although not as sensitive as the vulva itself.

ORGASM

Peak of sexual arousal (also known as a climax) producing feelings of intense physical and mental pleasure and contentment. In men it is accompanied by ejaculation of semen. Many women are capable of multiple orgasms, although some say they can enjoy sex without climaxing at all.

PERINEUM

Highly erogenous zone in both sexes located between anus and genitals.

PETTING

Any sexual touching that does not involve the genitals, such as embracing, kissing and caressing.

PILLOW

Pillows have many uses in lovemaking, such as padding for sensitive areas on hard or uneven surfaces, support in complicated positions, and to cushion falls during adventurous sex.

PROSTATE GLAND

Walnut-sized gland at the base of the male's bladder that produces some of the components of semen. Sometimes dubbed the "male G-spot", it can trigger a powerful sexual response when it is stimulated, for example, if a finger or sex toy is inserted in the anus.

REAR-ENTRY SEX

Also known as "doggy style", this is vaginal or anal intercourse that is performed with the woman's back towards her partner. Different versions include the "donkey", in which the woman is on all fours.

SAFER SEX

Any sexual activity that carries a low risk of transmitting sexual disease, including penetrative sex when using a condom and mutual masturbation. Each sex practice requires certain precautions.

SERVANTE D'AMOUR

Rear-entry position in which the woman kneels on the bed with her hands clasped behind her neck and supports her upper body on her elbows. Her partner kneels behind her and places his hands on her upper back for support. This is a highly submissive role for the woman, which can excite both partners.

SEX GAMES

Any fun activity with a sexual element. This can take the form of card games (strip poker), board games, where the loser pays a sexual forfeit, or role play such as fantasy, fancy dress or play fighting. Establish clear rules at the start and keep to them.

SHOWER

A shower nozzle played over erogenous zones can provide erotic stimulation in the bath or shower. Do not focus the water directly into any bodily orifices, as this can be very dangerous.

SPINNER

Adventurous and novel sexual sequence in which the man lies on his back while his partner starts off sitting astride him. She slowly turns herself around until she is facing in the opposite direction. This allows her to vary the pace and angle of penetration.

SPOONS

Position that combines side-by-side and rear-entry sex. It helps slow the pace of sex, while leaving the man's hands free to stroke his partner's breasts and genitals.

STANDING SLING

Form of standing sex where the woman lifts one leg and her partner supports it with his arm. This makes the woman's vagina more accessible.

TIES AND SCARVES

These are useful aids for bondage sex games. The tie can be used to render your partner helpless, and the scarf to blindfold them so they can't see what you are going to do next. This offers plenty of scope for sexual teasing and so heightens arousal.

U-SPOT

Highly sexually responsive region of the vulva that is located around the entrance to the urethra (the tube that passes urine out of the body).

VULVA

Collective term for a female's external genitals. It includes the labia majora/minora, clitoris and vaginal opening (vestibule).

WHEELBARROW

Rear-entry standing position in which the man holds his partner's legs at either side of his waist.

ZIPPER SEX

Oral sex performed on a man without him needing to remove his trousers.

INDEX

CREDITS

Publisher's Acknowledgements
Dressing-up clothes and sex toys courtesy of Harmony
Limited, 103 Oxford Street, London W1D 2HF

Author's Acknowledgements
The author would like to thank Aimee and Leah for their help,
advice and invaluable insights into the modern woman's mind.